Real Estate Investing for Beginners

Table of Contents

PREFACE ***6***

CHAPTER 1: INTRODUCTION **10**

CHAPTER 2: INVESTOR IN REAL ESTATE **12**

   2.1 Introduction 12

   2.2 Criteria 16

   2.3 Terms 19

   2.4 Network 22

   2.5 The Growth's Four Stages 27

CHAPTER 3: UNDERSTANDING THE EIGHT MYTHS IN REAL ESTATE **34**

   3.1 Myth 1 38

   3.2 Myth 2 45

   3.3 Myth 3 49

   3.4 Myth 4 58

   3.5 Myth 5 60

3.6 Myth 6 62

3.7 Myth 7 65

3.8 Myth 8 69

CHAPTER 4: MODELS IN REAL ESTATE..80

4.1 The Financial Model 80
    4.1.1 Equity Development 84
    4.1.2 Development in Cash Flow 91
    4.1.3 The Financial Journey........................... 94

4.2 The Network Model 107
    4.2.1 Your Inner Circle 118
    4.2.2 Your Support Circle............................ 121
    4.2.3 Your Service Circle 124
    4.2.4 Operating your Work Network 127
    4.2.5 Work Network Maintenance............... 130
    4.2.6 Work Network Engagement 135

4.3 The Lead Generation Model 142
    4.3.1 Location 154
    4.3.2 Type... 157
    4.3.3 Economic 160

4.4 The Acquisition Model 163
    4.4.1 Cash Flow and Equity......................... 167
    4.4.2 Buying and Selling Terms 173

CHAPTER 5: HOW TO RAISE FINANCING AND CAPITAL 181

5.1 Recognizing Capital Sources 181

5.2 Property Purchases Financing 193

5.3 Best Mortgage Financing 203

CHAPTER 6: PROPERTIES IDENTIFICATION AND EVALUATION 215

6.1 Value of Location 215

6.2 Leases and Property Valuation 227

6.3 Property Inspections, Due Diligence, and Closing 239

6.4 Making an Offer 252

CHAPTER 7: MYTH OF TENS 264

7.1 Increasing Property's Value by Ten Ways 264

7.2 Investing Success in Real Estate by Ten Ways 278

CHAPTER 8: GOALS TO REACHING TOP 287

8.1 Ascertain the Base Camp **287**
8.2 Protecting Future **292**
8.3 Future Funding **297**
8.4 Staying at Course **302**
CONCLUSION......................................305

PREFACE

This book is about the plans that make huge cash. On the other hand that I've mastered anything in my innovative vocation, it's this: Small plans, best case scenario yield little outcomes, and huge plans best case scenario beat little plans. In this way, when I need enormous outcomes, I need a major arrangement. The best results—in any of life's undertakings—are quite often the aftereffect of a major arrangement fueled by constant exertion over the long run. That approach won't just give you the most ideal opportunity to win; it will likewise place you in the most ideal position to win huge. Regarding making monetary riches—huge cash—a standout amongst the most ideal ways I've seen, one that is genuinely open to anybody, is to put resources into land. Land investing can be a marvelous road to riches. It can completely transform you and your family's future. Truth be told, it can furnish you with the essentials you need as well as the maximums you merit. This book isn't about your essentials; it's about your maximums your greatest potential as an investor.

Regardless of whether you are a learner or a prepared land investor, this book was composed for you. It was composed to enable you to succeed and succeed huge. All you need is an arrangement, a great arrangement—a demonstrated enormous arrangement that can direct you from the earliest starting point to the most abnormal amounts of investing. The Real Estate Investor will impart that arrangement to you. We need you to turn into a fruitful land investor, to accomplish your objectives, to succeed and prosper after some time, and even—should you so pick—to turn into a Real Estate Investor.

CHAPTER 1: INTRODUCTION

Real estate is one of the most sublime approaches for individuals of different economic means in order to create wealth. You should be competent for making an annualized return on at least 8 to 10% per year in order to invest in real estate over the decades. It is a phenomenon that investing in real estate is not a myth but needs some homework. You are more likely to end up with inferior properties or to overpay if you are sloppy doing your legwork. Our book apparently portrays how to purchase the best properties at a reasonable price. You can lose money, specifically in the short-term even though you should make money by investing in good real estate properties over the long-term period. Perhaps, do not unrealistically anticipate real estate values to accelerate every year. In the local real estate, declines might develop temporary purchasing opportunities. The occasional practice downturns should be only increased on an otherwise beneficial journey when you invest in real estate for the long-term period.

CHAPTER 2: INVESTOR IN REAL ESTATE

2.1 Introduction

A life-changing universal principle was documented in the latter 1940s named as "vital few and trivial many". The notion was that the comparatively minute extent of your attempts leads to the massive number of your outcomes. This notion is also based on 80:20 Rule of Vilfredo Pareto, who embraced that 20 percent of the population owns 80 percent of the wealth in their respective country. The notion that 80 percent of your outcomes can be led by 20 percent of your actions might be one of the most sublime principles you can adopt for your life. It is merely to extract the major from your effort and time. It is having a firm focus. It is to maximize your outcomes. It is a divine phenomenon that your efforts, experience or even natural ability cannot lead to your results, but a firm focus can play a vital role in your great success. You can explore the highest successors in any field and you will realize that they have a precise and firm focus; just as important, you will discover that their focus was based on the right things: the handful of truly substantial issues that make the major difference. They realize what matters to them and when it matters most. You too will achieve that desired level of focus as you move toward becoming a successful real estate investor. Over time they will grow significantly even though the outcomes that emerge from that focus might initiate sluggishly.

The goal of high achievers was to quest the basic notions they focused on a day in and day out regardless of any disruption in the real estate investment world. In which realms did they struggle to be substantiated? What we identified is that these high achievers have focused on three fundamental but realistically firm forces of real estate investing at the heart. It is a fact that these three forces are at the prime of all investing, which include Criteria, Terms, and networks. We have come to identify to them fundamentally as CTN or "Dynamic Trio of Investing".

2.2 Criteria

A criterion is the first principle of the CTN or "Dynamic Trio of Investing". It describes what you purchase. They are the benchmarks that demonstrate what sort of property you are looking for. The criteria you emphasized are the aspects you usually write on your all properties bulletin (APB) when you are searching for the latter chance. Is the property a single-family or a multi-family? What is development? Does it possess the appropriate aspects and services that make it accountable for rental or resale? Most importantly, where an investment is located? Your criteria are the things of the property that are based on unchallengeable facts, the things that cannot be ignored anyway. They are a fundamental aspect of your investment tactic.

The choices to the properties of an investor are narrowed using Criteria that highlight the major chance as well as the minimal risk practically. What you get in return is something with forecasted value, when the desired property matches your criteria. When you think your criteria as an opportunity screen, it allows you to keep out the bad and retains the good. Bad criteria have been the decline of many potential investors as such good criteria are the backbone of successful real estate investing. Later on, we will discuss the particular Criteria highest achievers or successful investors utilize to choose their investment properties in this book. Criteria are fundamental regarding realizing forecasted value as well as that is why they are the first realm of focus for the successful investor of the highest achievers.

2.3 Terms

Terms describe how you switch opportunity into a deal if criteria describe it. Terms realize its value to you either in present or in the future once a property meets your criteria. Terms include everything from the offered price, interest rate to conveyances, closing costs, occupancy, and down payment and; therefore, are the negotiable things of a purchase. Terms are most purposeful and beneficial for every investor as they can make a great deal using the most modest criteria. Skillful negotiation of Terms can drive to enhanced cash flow, a better equity position, and sometimes both. It is about how close a transaction, how much money you need to achieve property, and how much the property will possess over time. The purpose of terms is to emphasize the realm of focus and to maximize financial value for the real estate investor.

We will be discussing the key Terms of any investment that can make the major difference in the comparative success of a transaction. Always note, you do not have to be a gifted investor for capitalizing on terms.

It is regarding understand the financial basics of a transaction, to know the flexible elements, and being systematic regarding acquire all you can from every deal. It is also rewarding to know when to walk away. Remember, you have not to go out but you must make your money going in. let the market go to work for you as opposed to buy less as compared to the right and hope the market will save you when you buy the right. Purchasing right refers to get the right Terms.

2.4 Network

The network is the last member of the Dynamic Trio. The network of investors assists them in their investing. The network is a surprise contender when we attempt to pin down the important realms that make the major difference in real estate investment. The major dilemma is that investors do not see it coming. The notion of the personal entrepreneurial investor beat the streets for dealing with the perceptions brought to the mind of most individuals. However, repeatedly, investors preferred to all the individuals who assisted them to succeed throughout the inquiry. In many cases, they had associations with individuals who sent those chances, assisted them in buying and maintaining their properties, mentored them, and offered services that allowed them to do more while investing less effort and time. We even can this leverage in the context of a businessperson, which shows the fact that they can achieve more with experienced assistance as compared to achieve alone.

We will assist you being investors in understanding how to ascertain a "dream group" for your investment career when we review comprehensively about Network in later sections. It is a fact that you will need assistance from real estate agents to contractors. Indeed, the network will come first in your investing career as you will depend on those individuals to assist get your investment career launched reliably, profitably, and safely even though the network is the last of the three items we explored. The information and suggestion provided to you in these pages will assist you in selecting the most beneficial and work successfully with them over time.

The questions of what you will purchase, who will help you, and how you will buy it are answered from the three realms of focus for the real estate investor based on the Criteria, Terms, and Network. Most important, Criteria explore, Terms identify, and your Network encourages all the spending you do. Successfully understanding these realms will provide you the better opportunity for lasting success as well as place you comprehensively on the platform to become a real estate investor.

2.5 The Growth's Four Stages

Four stages of growth progress the platform of a real estate investor. Firstly, before you make your first move, you must learn to think like a real estate investor or for a million. Your experience can teach you that the bigger you think, the more I can achieve whether this allows you as a timeless truth or as a formula. You have to understand that what you hold in your mind is what shows you up in your life. The greatest change to become one will be given from the understanding of thinking like a real estate investor.

Buy a million is the next step in which you will acquire a major understanding of the effective models to invest in real estate and thinking of money, more basic. The objective is to employ you with the operating models you require to buy investment properties with a market value of a million dollars or more. This is not a massive jump you can realize as well as a number of investors acquire that benchmark long before they ever anticipated they would, believe it or not. In some cases, purchasing a million is regarding the basics of equipping properties, possessing them, and selling them. The strength of Criteria, Terms, and Network is applied for launching your career in order to invest purchase a million.

After you "Buy a Million", you will set your focus on having a value position of a million dollars or more in your properties. We consider this stage Own a Million. This is the point at which you will understand that the putting you have done has bloomed into a genuine business. With that change come to a lot of issues explicit to that dimension of possession. Obtaining properties through credit conceivably turns out to be increasingly troublesome, money turns into aware, and dealing with your investments could require help from a few quarters. This stage includes managing and frequently offsetting income with resources or value development. It might include selling, exchanging up, or trading. It surely includes understanding the shockingly straightforward substances of assessment and proprietor element issues. Fortunately, by understanding these issues from the earliest starting point, you can get ready for them. That is the thing that the models in this book are proposed to enable you to do. By starting with the correct models, demonstrated ones that can deal with the enormous issues, you'll never need to stop and scratch your head or, more regrettable, begin once again and rethink what you do.

The last phase of development for a Real Estate Investor is "Get a Million". Consider it the summit, a spot where just the best have gone. Get a Million is a point at which you are in a condition to get a yearly salary of a million dollars from your investments. Essential to this stage is that your investment business is planned with the goal that you can escape the everyday work and appreciate the advantages of what you've made. In spite of the fact that you can venture out anytime en route, it will be your expectation that you will focus on a major objective.

Precisely when you choose to move into the "get mode" it is up to you. Clearly, you don't need to hold up until you're accepting a million dollars per year. As a portion of the financial specialists we met in our exploration, you can acknowledge the income you've manufactured and ventured out of the business sooner. On the other hand, you can pause and get progressively down the line. The fact of the matter is that on the off chance that you've pursued the models of The Real Estate Investor, you will have more options, and that is a generally amazing thing to have in your budgetary riches building life.

CHAPTER 3: UNDERSTANDING THE EIGHT MYTHS IN REAL ESTATE

When asking with individuals about investing, what frequently turns out to be clear is that they don't at first perceive that anxiety or uncertainty is assuming a huge job in their monetary lives. They feel that contributing is essentially an erudite choice they have or haven't exploited. While they can recognize the benefit of investing, they can't exactly legitimize why they aren't doing it all regularly or by any means. The best money related rewards more than likely will be found outside their usual ranges of familiarity. That is the point at which they at long last comprehend that feelings of anxiety and questions undermine their certainty and their activities and at last can drive a ground-breaking section among them and their fantasies.

Truth be told, there is a capacity to distinguish eight of those restricting myths that would-be investors generally hold about turning into a financial specialist and about investing itself. Everybody who expects to turn out to be financially well-off will manage them at some point or another. It all of a sudden ended up that these questions don't leave without anyone else; left un-inspected or not managed, they can protect you from turning into an extraordinary investor. Individuals; by and large, have two different ways of taking a look at anything: the manner in which they see themselves on the planet and the manner in which they see the world and how it functions. You may figure it would be turned around that your impression of how the world functions would educate your sense regarding how effective you could be yet, strangely enough, it isn't. The picture you have of yourself as a financial specialist turns into the focal point through which you see the universe of investing, and that mental self-portrait will either control or mislead you. Curiously, any experts you have about yourself as a financial specialist will, in general, amplify your mistaken assumptions about investing.

3.1 Myth 1

It is practically prevalent what number of individuals figure they don't should be an investor. Generally, that happens on the grounds that they accept deliberately or unknowingly that the way to money related riches is through one's occupation. In case you're similar to me and trust that monetary riches are tied in with having enough unmerited pay to fund your life mission without the need to work, odds are your present place of employment salary and investment funds plan won't be sufficiently about to construct genuine budgetary riches. It is exceedingly far-fetched that your activity makes enough salary for you to set aside a sensible level of it and, at a normal rate of intrigue, still accomplish genuine money related riches.

Thrifty people would stash little entireties of cash in espresso jars, under sleeping cushions, and in close to home investment accounts, trusting, in the long run, would accomplish money related opportunity. In increasingly present day times this "unobtrusive saver" has developed into the "humble financial specialist."

In all actuality, just a small level of individuals, most likely under 1 percent, make enough salary from their business to turn out to be monetarily well off. I'm discussing individuals, for example, generously compensated competitors, on-screen characters, performers, and officials. The uncommon pay these individuals get is large to the point that they effectively could live off a small amount of their salary, contribute the rest, and even with unobtrusive rates of return accomplish budgetary riches. The usable word here is can. I'm persistently stunned at what number of these high salary makers figure they don't should be financial specialists.

I urge you to take a gander at your specific type of employment in an unexpected way. Your activity is where you can acquire your underlying investment capital, and a level of your wages must be devoted to working up your investment stake. I would prefer not to stun you, however, the unbelievable financial specialist Sir John Templeton recounts to the tale of how he and his significant other lived off as meager as 50 percent of their salary toward the start of his investment vocation. They made a round of perceiving how well they could live on just a small amount of their family unit salary.

In a perfect world, you should take a gander at your work along these lines: It can be an energy that pays you cash for doing what you want to do. A few interests pay more than others, however as history demonstrates, they seldom pay enough to make money related freedom. Your activity is your activity;

money related to riches building is something different. That is the manner by which I think Sorenson took a gander at it, and I urge you to do something very similar.

The vast majority imagine that procuring cash in occupation and sparing some of it or staying in the organization retirement plan makes them investors. It doesn't—however, they figure it does or thinks it is close enough that they don't should be a financial specialist. It is this Myth Understanding that causes numerous individuals not to turn out to be genuine financial specialists. Try not to give that a chance to be you. Understand that whatever your activity or work is, you likewise should be an investor. You should get up in the first part of the day letting yourself know, "I'm an investor. I'm building budgetary riches. The present the day I could discover a chance and make an arrangement!"

3.2 Myth 2

You have no clue what you will need or need past today. You can't foresee what life will offer not far off for good or for awful. As hard as you may attempt, you can't foresee with any certainty the assets you'll have to manage life's vulnerabilities. Confounding everything is the way that it requires investment to develop cash. Money related riches building isn't something that can be practiced in response mode. It is extremely hard to discover more cash since all of you of an unexpected need or needs it. As I've said from the start, little cash comes effectively—huge cash does not. Turning into an investor—somebody who seeks after money related riches constructing each day—is tied in with getting ready for the essentials and maximums throughout your life: the capricious budgetary essentials you may require and the unexpected monetary maximums you may need. In the event that you decide not to seek after money related riches, your future more than likely will be characterized by incredibly constraining monetary decisions. You may need to scramble to meet your changing needs or manage without the things you, in the long run, wish for. At a point in your life when making do with less may decimate you, you may need to do only that.

To begin with, there are the individuals who (since they decided not to assemble monetary riches) have restricted chances to think about themselves and their friends and family. Second, there are the individuals who (since they sought after money related riches as a financial specialist) have a lot bigger chances to think about themselves and their friends and family yet in addition for a great deal more. It's the contrast between attention on the essentials life can require and an emphasis on the maximums life can offer. It comes down to what sort of individual you need to be and the existence you need to lead.

3.3 Myth 3

I truly battle with along these lines of reasoning. I simply don't comprehend why individuals appear to need to put judgment in front of exertion and dubious assessments before a readiness to attempt. There's no chance to get for you, or any other individual so far as that is concerned, to know your actual monetary potential. Also, on the grounds that your actual money related potential is obscure, it looks bad as far as possible on it. "I can't do it" turns into another basis for not attempting, for not extending, for not investigating your potential. A few people have revealed to me they would prefer not to set themselves up for disillusionment. The heartbreaking incongruity is that the general population who might rather not set themselves up for dissatisfaction by putting it all on the line are the extremely ones bound for disillusionment. The minute you get tied up with the possibility that you can't accomplish a money-related riches, you put yourself on the way to lack of concern, bargain, and, at last, lament.

As far as I can tell there are fundamentally two different ways individuals see their money-related potential. There are the individuals who think regarding what's monetarily plausible and the individuals who think as far as what's monetarily conceivable. Likelihood scholars base their perspective on their future budgetary selves on their previous history and current abilities. They state to themselves, "In view of individual identity and my identity, this is most likely what I can monetarily achieve later on." They use words, for example, sensible and likely when they examine their money-related potential. Thus, when they are given another open door that doesn't accommodate the assumptions of their money-related potential, they frequently infer that they basically "can't do it." For them, their budgetary future is resolved, unsurprising, and at last static.

Conceivable outcomes scholars, interestingly, infrequently articulate the words "I can't do it." They put aside any restricting thoughts they may have about their money-related potential and base their perspective on their future budgetary selves on what they envision themselves to be fit for achieving. What's more, they utilize a by and large extraordinary vocabulary their potential is depicted as far as what's "possible," what's "believable," and what's "conceivable." They state to themselves: "I have dreams about which areas it should be. In light of who I can turn into, this is the thing that I can monetarily achieve." They consider that they may need to adopt new things, gain new abilities, or change their propensities to achieve their full monetary potential. For them, their budgetary future is adaptable, dynamic, and, eventually, alive.

When individuals venture over into plausibility considering and trust that they can accomplish budgetary riches, they frequently observe an entirely different arrangement of snags. They rapidly turned into sure that they will require additional time, cash, and investment information than they at present have or could procure effectively. They think things like "It's past the point of no return, I don't have sufficient opportunity," "It is extremely unlikely; I simply don't have enough cash to begin investing," or "I would on the off chance that I could, however, I have no clue what to do, what's more, I'm nothing more than a bad memory with cash." What these people don't understand is that most enormous things begin little.

While numerous individuals erroneously trust they need a great deal of every one of the three, they really need a tad bit of each: the correct capacities, well-invested energy, and well-put cash. Past this, they can quicken their development as a financial specialist by picking one zone to increment. They can concentrate on procuring greater capacity (through perusing, workshops, or guides), give it the additional time, or pull in more cash.

Your self-appraisal in these three territories regularly directs your methodology. Individuals who have the advantage of time yet have constrained money related assets can concentrate on intensifying their capacity to make more prominent progress. They additionally can win sweat value by doing a great part of the work different financial specialists may contract out. Conversely, investors with progressively money related assets and less time can stand to utilize specialists and temporary workers to compensate for their absence of time. Time and cash frequently are firmly associated, in that time can be utilized to acquire cash and cash can be invested to purchase energy.

3.4 Myth 4

Investing is confounded. Be that as it may, to be reasonable, nearly anything, taken all in all, can seem more confused than it truly is. All you need to know are the fundamental principles of the street and how to drive. Investing is the same. Try to venture back and recognize the angles that issue the most.

On a functional premise, what I can be sure of is that you never need to know everything so as to accomplish something. You simply need to know the right activities at a random minute. After some time, given enough opportunities to study and experience something, you normally and logically will get the hang of all that you have to know to do it well. That is the manner in which you become a specialist. Land investing is the same. When you learn things in the right request, your insight will come all the more effectively and all the more rapidly.

3.5 Myth 5

One of the extraordinary exercises I've found out about investing is this: Investing in what you don't have the foggiest idea or comprehend isn't investing in any way. Doing that resembles making a go in obscurity, and you'll require karma to hit anything beneficial, substantially less your expected target. To me, the genuine idea of investing is dependable to put resources into what you know and completely get it. Pick a territory that you definitely know or one that incredibly interests you and subscribes to turning into a specialist in it after some time. Here is an investor who totally, regardless of what the obvious upside is, adheres to his criteria. I urge you to do something very similar; in the event that you don't have particular information, pick a territory and begin adapting today. I think you'll find that investing in land is one of the simplest regions of investing in which to get master learning and comprehension.

3.6 Myth 6

In the event that you gaze upward "contribute" in the dictionary, this is the thing that you'll discover: "Contribute—to submit (cash or capital) so as to pick up a monetary return." You'll see that "hazard" doesn't show up anyplace in the definition. Why? Since a hazard is a thing that individuals convey to the idea of investing. I would prefer not to seem like a Pollyanna, yet truly extraordinary investors don't consider investing dangerous. For them it's not tied in with disregarding hazard; rather, it's tied in with following sound investment standards and models.

Much of the time this implies purchasing something of significant worth for terms that quickly make a benefit for you. Along these lines, investors go into the arrangement realizing they needn't bother with the market to safeguard them out. These are the "no-hazard" bargains. Investing like a Real Estate Investor isn't tied in with going out on a limb. It is tied in with having sound criteria, the persistence to locate the correct chance, and a readiness to make the right move rapidly.

The best financial specialists know this and are devoted to following this recipe. Thus, they are continually limiting their hazard while amplifying their arrival. Investing can never be totally hazarded free, yet it doesn't need to be unsafe.

3.7 Myth 7

Timing is everything. However at this point you realize that, overlook it, since you can't genuinely time anything. Timing is a standout amongst the most misconstrued ideas in investing. At the point when individuals state that planning is significant, they are right. Timing isn't just significant; it's basic to investment achievement. The economy is patterned. Markets are patterned. Also, purchasing and selling openings are made by the back and forth movement of the cycles. Finding the best time to purchase or sell is called timing. What is misconstrued is the manner in which timing really is cultivated. The vast majority contemplate dynamic perception—sitting on the sidelines hanging tight for the minute when they should bounce in and make a move. It's an uninvolved and afterward dynamic methodology. At the end of the day, timing is tied in with being receptive to circumstance. Reality, notwithstanding, is that planning is tied in with being dynamic—dynamic constantly. I trust that by far most of chances can't be seen from the sidelines—you should be in the diversion. The best arrangements originate from the best chances, and the best open doors go quick. This is the place the expression "a fateful opening" originates from. Investors perceive and catch these open doors since they are constantly occupied with the amusement and near the activity.

Fruitful planning is made conceivable by time invested on the assignment over energy. You need to keep your snare in the water. Being dynamic and drawn in doesn't mean you're continually purchasing and selling. What it means is that you are reliably looking with your Criteria, careful for the minute when opportunity surfaces. This is the thing that I mean when I state that planning discovers you. You can never realize the most perfect time to act with the exception of sometime later. Knowing the past is, as it's been said, 20/20. Better to see it like this: Any time an open door meets your exacting Criteria and you act, you have planned the market effectively. Timing isn't tied in with being in the ideal spot at the ideal time; it's tied in with being in the ideal spot constantly.

3.8 Myth 8

Rest guaranteed: All the wise investments will be taken. The main inquiry is by whom. As straightforward as it sounds, in all actuality the individuals who take them are the individuals who best comprehend the conditions that make them. Coincidentally, this is the other and progressively unpretentious side of the planning issue. While the recently examined legend was tied in with timing the market, this fantasy tends to your planning as an investor. It appears as though the couple of chances I've had the option to discover are now taken." I comprehend what they're stating, and there are extremely two issues at work here: the possibility that there aren't numerous arrangements and the possibility that you're past the point where it is possible to get them. This is what I think about market powers and how they make investment openings. There are two major powers at work—financial ones and individual ones—and they are constantly present, dependably at work, and continually affecting the commercial center. Fundamental financial powers appear as things, for example, work development, loan fees, populace movements, and region rejuvenation. These are the things the vast majority considers when they think about the powers that make investment openings. What is regularly neglected, in any case, is a second arrangement of human, or individual, powers that are constantly present and can make extra and huge investment openings. Some emerge from positive conditions, for example, movement, marriage, and family development. Others emerge from negative conditions, for example, separation, passing, and obligation. As far as I can tell, the individuals who proclaim that all the great arrangements are taken are quite often neglecting this second arrangement of human powers and the novel open doors they make. What I most need you to comprehend is that open doors are dependably there in each market and in without fail. Some of the time there are a great deal, and now and again there are most certainly not. A few open doors are the consequence of clear monetary powers. Others are the aftereffect of nearby and accidental individual powers. Also, you're never past the point of no return. Since individual powers are dependably at work, these open doors are always being made. While yesterday's arrangements have for sure been taken, tomorrow's arrangements have not; nor are they bound to go consequently to another person. In any case, in time they will be taken by somebody, and I need you to understand that somebody could be you. It's extremely a round of covering up and looks for, and in the event that you pick, you are presently "it" and must look for. The open doors are gone just for the individuals who accept they are. You're past the point of no return just on the off chance that you accept you're past the point of no return.

All things considered, let me urge you to trust that everything huge begins little. At the point when a great many people think about investing out of the blue, it isn't extraordinary for them to figure, "It will take everlastingly for my investments to add up to anything." When they think about their first investment, the vast majority think that it's hard to legitimize the time, cash, and exertion for the profits they can see. It can appear franticness to look so hard for an investment property that may yield just a few hundred dollars per month. These momentary advantages simply don't appear to adjust the transient penances. I emphatically urge you to venture past that transient reasoning and take a gander at the bigger ramifications of little investments. What must be comprehended is that there is a characteristic development bend to force. Think about a ball moving downhill that grabs mass and speed as it goes. It's what we ordinarily call the snowball impact. In spite of the fact that it might begin little or moderate, it winds up becoming very huge and quick. Similarly, cash, once contributed, has its own force, and the specialized name for that is "exacerbating." What begins little and develops gradually gathers in size and speed after some time.

Any type of investing is tied in with giving your cash something to do and giving it a chance to work for you after some time. Land investing is the same. What recognizes it from different investments is that the first estimation of your advantage will in general be substantial and, through the enchantment of influence, can be bought for less. For instance, on the off chance that you purchased a $100,000 investment house every year by putting $10,000 down and accomplished just an unobtrusive 5 percent rate of profit for the all-out estimation of the benefits, you'd be a tycoon in less than 10 years. With every benefit you add to your portfolio, your portfolio develops. As your investments develop, so do your purchasing power and your investment learning. That is the establishment for greater and regularly expanding investments.

Regardless of what your present station in life is, monetary riches are accessible to you. Regardless of how minimal expenditure or information you have initially, an incredible closure is workable for you. Try to begin and afterward let the intensity of development on development take you higher. The longest voyages are only an aggregation of little advances; the tallest structures are worked by setting obstruct upon square. In case you're prepared to make the following stride on your adventure to budgetary riches, on the off chance that you trust that it is both conceivable and plausible for you, it's an ideal opportunity to desert your Myth Understandings, turn the page, and start having a similar outlook as a Real Estate Investor.

CHAPTER 4: MODELS IN REAL ESTATE

4.1 The Financial Model

There are two different ways to manufacture budgetary riches by investing in land. I realize that sounds excessively basic, however it's valid: There are only two. Inside those two are huge bandages of varieties that can give the presence of enormous multifaceted nature, and by utilizing those different alternatives you can make land investing as intricate as you need. They generally begin with the fundamentals and work from that point. When you genuinely comprehend the two essential drivers of monetary riches, you start to see the principal openings they present and skill to exploit them. In the event that you resemble me or any of our Millionaire Real Estate Investors, this is the point at which you truly get energized. That is the intensity of this money related model—it aides you and inspires you. The two different ways to profit in land investing, the two drivers of monetary riches, are Equity Buildup and Cash Flow Growth. They can happen at the same time, thus you can profit by both in the meantime. Value Buildup expands your total assets in your land resources, while Cash Flow Growth gives a surge of unmerited pay. You can live on that salary or reinvest it by squaring away your obligation or securing all the more land. In the event that you keep your cash in play by reinvesting the Cash Flow, you are quickening your Equity Buildup and accordingly the development of your own total assets. Keep in mind, your total assets is the proportion of your prosperity—your score in the round of budgetary riches building.

4.1.1 Equity Development

When you take a gander at Equity Buildup attentively, you find that it originates from two variables: value gratefulness and obligation pay down. On the off chance that you get it right, your land investment will start with an edge of value immediately. This implies your underlying up front installment (Investment) in addition to the home loan advance you acquire (Debt), when included, will even now be not exactly the value you could sell the property for (Market Value). That distinction is your value in the property.

After some time, as you lease the property, the two characteristic powers of cost thankfulness and obligation pay down cooperate to build your value. Clearly, if the market esteem expands, your value in the property goes up; however it likewise goes up in light of the fact that you are squaring away the obligation through the home loan. Every regularly scheduled installment you make lessens the sum you owe on the advance. Consequently, as the home loan obligation diminishes over the term of the advance (30 years, 15 years, and so on.), your value increases reliably.

We should take an actual example for this procedure. In the event that you had put resources into a private pay property in 1988 at the then middle home cost of around $90,000, it would, after 15 years, in 2003, have been worth nearly $170,000. Value thankfulness would have picked up you $81,000 in value. You additionally would have been satisfying the home loan and along these lines paying off your obligation.

This count of obligation pay down requires some painstakingly thought about suspicions. To begin with, it expect that you acquired the property at 20 percent underneath market esteem ($90,000 20 percent $72,000); second, it accept that you made a 20 percent up front installment (20 percent $72,000 = $14,400). This implies you would have gotten a home loan advance of $57,600 ($72,000 $14,400 = $57,600). As you make your month to month advance installments, secured by the rental salary from your inhabitants, you are satisfying some bit of the credit's outstanding parity and along these lines paying off your obligation on the property. As you pay off the obligation, you increment your value. In this genuine model, with a credit of $57,600 and an average 30-year contract, you would have, amid those 15 years, paid off the advance obligation to $43,334 and hence increased another $14,266 in value development. The shorter the length of the advance is, the quicker you will accomplish obligation pay down. In the precedent we are utilizing, a 15-year home loan would have paid off the obligation to $0 and accordingly expanded the value by the full $57,600 measure of the advance.

What makes the Financial Model of the Millionaire Real Estate Investor so convincing is the joined effect of every one of these components. This is the place the influence of land to construct budgetary riches is completely uncovered. In the investment we have broken down, this is the means by which everything includes: Your $14,400 investment in 1988 transformed into value of more than $128,506 in only 15 years. This would resemble putting your $14,400 in a financial balance paying a yearly aggravated loan fee of 15.7 percent. On the off chance that you had utilized a 15-year contract rather than a 30-year contract, your value would have developed to more than $171,840. That resembles a yearly exacerbated loan cost of 17.9 percent. In either case this is a noteworthy rate of profitability and not one you will discover at a bank. What's more, those surprising returns don't reflect what happens when you factor for Cash Flow Growth.

4.1.2 Development in Cash Flow

In the same class as this Equity Buildup is, it isn't the entire story. There is the additional advantage of Cash Flow Growth to consider. Net Cash Flow is accomplished from a land investment when the rental salary you get is more than the costs you bring about. The expenses incorporate your costs, a recompense for opening, and obligation administration For now allows simply state that on the off chance that you get it right, account it admirably, and control your costs, you can accomplish a positive Net Cash

Flow. As rents increase in value over time, the income will develop. When the advance is satisfied, the Net Cash Flow develops significantly in light of the fact that your month to month contract credit installment leaves. In our case of the $90,000 investment property bought in 1988, we reasonably could have gotten over the 15 years a complete Net Cash Flow between $18,000 and $34,000. In 2004, our sixteenth year of proprietorship, the yearly Net Cash Flow from the property would be about $4,600 with the 30-year contract. On account of the

15-year credit, since it would be satisfied, our yearly Net Cash Flow would hop to over $9,400.

4.1.3 The Financial Journey

How about we perceive how the numbers play out. What happens when you make numerous land investments over various years? The clearest approach to see this is to pursue the way of a Real Estate Investor who started to contribute a few years back and afterward observe what might have happened to those investments. How about we start in 1983, track the advancement more than 20 years, and watch the numbers develop—both Equity Buildup and Cash Flow Growth. This multiyear take a gander at the Financial

Model will recount to an anecdote about the voyage of somebody who started his or her land investing in 1983. For the story suppose that individual was you. With you as our model land investor, we will see what you did more than 20 years and how it turned out. We will find how you had the option to transform an underlying investment of $11,248 into a value position of over $1.6 million and a yearly net income of over $50,000. How could you do this from 1983 to 2002? It is an interesting and uncovering story—a practical and energizing voyage of budgetary riches building. It is the account of turning into a Real Estate Investor.

Everything started when you pursued the shrewd exhortation of your tutor to "get it appropriate." With that counsel as your guide, every one of the 15 investments you made amid those 20 years was in the "center of the market," at about the middle home cost, acquired at 20 percent beneath market value. Your first investment in 1983 was at the U.S. middle home cost of $70,300. You paid $56,240 for the property, contributed $11,248 (20 percent) as the upfront installment, and financed the remaining $44,992 with a 30-year contract credit. That turned into your basic recipe—middle value, 20 percent markdown, 20 percent down, and a 30-year advance. You remained consistent with that demonstrated recipe for the following 20 years. You realized that if land costs and leases acknowledged at a normal of around 5 percent a year as time goes on and that on the off chance that you utilized the best accessible financing (with a recorded normal loan cost of about 7.4 percent) and held your costs to around 40 percent of your rents, your value would construct thus would your net income. Actually, you anticipated that your absolute first investment property would, following 20 years, have a market estimation of over $180,000 and your value in the property would be more than $160,000. You were correct—that is in reality what occurred. In any case, for you that was just the start. Your guide informed you regarding the aggravating intensity of making a few land investments after some time. He said it would increase both your total assets and your easy revenue exponentially. In this manner, you kept on investing in land cautiously however reliably. Being reasonable and requiring time to amass a few reserve funds, you made your second investment two years after the fact in 1985. The middle cost had ascended to $75,500, and utilizing your recipe of a 20 percent rebate and 20 percent down, you procured the property with an initial installment of $12,080 and financed $48,320 with an additional 30-year credit. You kept actualizing your land investment technique by quietly sparing a portion of your earned salary and efficiently scanning for the following chance. You made it your objective to put resources into another private salary property like clockwork, purchasing your third property in 1987, your fourth in 1989, and your fifth in 1991. In this way, in only 10 years you possessed five properties.

You had put $67,960 of your reserve funds in five houses now worth over $537,000, and your value had developed to over $280,000. Your net yearly income previously surpassed $6,800—the greater part of what you put resources into your first house. You realized you could apply that income toward your next obtaining. Truth is told, since you had amassed over $33,297 in net income over the initial 10 years, you could now, in the event that you picked, make all your future yearly buys from that aggregated income. That collected cash, when added to your progressing yearly income, would more than spread all your future up front installments! Presently your story truly starts to get energizing. With your solid value position and expanding yearly income, you started in 1993 to secure an investment property every year for the following 10 years. In this manner, before the finish of 2002, your twentieth entire year as a land investor, you possessed 15 private pay properties. They have a consolidated market estimation of over $2.5 million, and you have value development of over $1.6 million. You have turned into a Millionaire Real Estate Investor with only 15 "get it right" acquisitions in just 20 years. Indeed, you really turned into a total assets land mogul three years before that, in 1999, with the 12 properties you claimed at that point.

Notwithstanding your $1.6 million in value toward the finish of 2002, you would have earned more than $303,000 in collected income. All that income could have been utilized to make your continuous land investments or to square away your advances, changing over the income straightforwardly to value. As you think back on your most recent 20 years, you understand that you have turned your all out $271,800 of down payments into an arrival on investment of more than $1.9 million. In the event that you did know all the more investing throughout the following five years, those 15 properties would be worth almost $3.3 million and your value would surpass $2.4 million. To really sweeten the deal, your yearly net income would be nearly $90,000. Not awful: 25 years, 15 properties, $2.4 million total assets, and $90,000 yearly income.

As should be obvious, these investors have a middle market estimation of $3.7 million for their investment properties, a value position of $1.5 million, and a yearly net income of $85,000. Our 20-year investment story, with 15 acquisitions from 1983 to 2002, produced

$1.6 million in value (essentially indistinguishable to the case for Millionaire Real Estate Investors) with a market estimation of $2.6 ($1 million not exactly those we met) and a yearly income of $50,500 (likewise not exactly our land moguls). The Real Estate Investors we met likewise had more obligations in their investments (60 percent versus the 38 percent in our story). No doubt they are purchasing bigger properties, most likely multifamily, and collecting more obligation yet more prominent income. We have been increasingly mindful and maybe moderate in applying this monetary model.

4.2 The Network Model

Nobody ever prevails without anyone else or herself—nobody. Behind each example of overcoming adversity is another example of overcoming adversity; behind each effective individual is a similarly fruitful individual. While the term independent is utilized regularly, the implicit certainty is that nobody is independent, regardless of whether organically, profoundly, physically, actually, expertly, or monetarily. In this way, check out you and know this: Millionaire investors aren't prevailing without the assistance of others. For each Real Estate Investor you may know, there is a gathering of individuals working off camera that helped cause or boost his or her prosperity. They are the mogul's Network—a deliberately selected gathering of individuals who each assume a key job in helping the Millionaire Real Estate Investor succeed. Investors couldn't prevail without this gathering. Neither can you. A Real Estate Investor's Network is an interconnected gathering of individuals with three things in like manner: They assume a functioning proficient job in land investments, they are the best at what they do, and they are eager to help you when you need assistance.

Try not to mistake this for your Leads Network. This is your Work Network. Albeit after some time you additionally will approach those individuals for leads and endeavor to incorporate them in your Leads Network, this isn't your essential explanation behind structure your Work Network. These are the general population who give you exhortation, direction, shrewdness, data, guidance, insight, information, tutoring, procedure, counsel, contacts, associations, drives, authority, influence, and work. Some additionally give joining forces when you need it and fair input notwithstanding when you don't. This Work Network is your own and key riches building relationship with others. It is the place you go to discover every one of the general population you have to discover, gain proficiency with every one of the things you have to know, and complete every one of the things you have to complete. To put it plainly, your Work Network is your investing help.

In any case, be cautious: It isn't simply anybody you need in your life saver. In the event that you have a fantasy, you will require a fantasy group. In the event that you have a major dream, you will require a major dream group. On the off chance that you have a major and ground-breaking dream to accomplish money related riches through land investing, you will require a major and ground-breaking dream group to accomplish it. You need individuals, the ideal individuals, to enable you to get what you need. In the event that you need to turn into a

Millionaire Real Estate Investor, you should unite a ground-breaking gathering of individuals, a fantasy group, who would all be able to assume the correct jobs at the correct occasions so you can accomplish your budgetary dreams. You need your own mogul land investing Work Network.

The individuals from your Work Network will give you a wide assortment of significant and interrelated things. They will help you from start to finish with your exchanges. They will illuminate and exhort you about what to do and what not to do. They will give the "best work" at the "best cost" in the "best time." They will be there when you truly need them—and no later.

On the off chance that you don't have a Work Network, you'll be working alone. Also, in the event that you ever need somebody, you'll need to take whoever you can get right now. You won't know whether you are getting the best counsel, best work, best cost, or best time. You'll simply know you're when absolutely necessary and can't do it without anyone else. Balance this with previously having this Network set up. You'll know the best, recognize what they charge, know when they can do it, and realize you can rely on them. You'll be toward the front of good choices rather than toward the back of urgent ones. You'll get what you need when you need it. You'll have the option to settle on incredible choices rapidly in light of the fact that you won't need to back off to go searching for individuals.

There is a commonsense motivation behind why they do this and a logical clarification for why it works. They encircle themselves with extraordinary individuals since they intend to be incredible investors who plan to accomplish more than one arrangement. They intend to copy their prosperity many occasions after some time. To do that, they need to effectively, intentionally, and specifically assemble amazing working connections that are long haul and commonly useful. They are making a hover of impact with themselves at the middle. Tycoons don't simply look for powerful individuals—they become compelling.

There's a logical motivation behind why this works. When you are making your very own circles of impact, you're really pulling individuals toward you and your objectives. You're making a genuine power of nature. It's known as a centripetal power. The word centripetal is from the Latin for "focus chasing" and alludes to any power that coordinates objects toward the focal point of a circle. In their reality Millionaire Real Estate Investors are such a power. They purposefully draw in the perfect individuals into their circles of impact and force them in close around them. They are a focal point of impact.

In view of this we need you to complete two things: Visualize yourself encompassed by incredible individuals and begin running in the correct circles to draw in and keep them. When you're clear about what you need your monetary life to seem as though, you'll be clear about who you'll have to encircle yourself with and what you'll have to do to pull in those individuals. We need you to be deliberate in your work connections and never settle.

4.2.1 Your Inner Circle

Your Inner Circle is made out of the key individuals who completely and really care about your budgetary achievement. No uncertainties, and, or buts about it—they are focused on you. These are the general population nearest to you; the select gathering you trust the most. Every one of them ought to have greater investment learning, knowledge, and accomplishment than you have and be happy to coach and guide you. Consider them your casual directorate for riches building and land investment choices—your very own Millionaire Mastermind. What isolates the individuals from your Inner Circle from every other person isn't their main thing for you expertly yet what they accomplish for you by and by. On the off chance that you don't have a clue what to do, they'll let you know or discover somebody who can. On the off chance that you need assistance, they will furnish it or interface you with somebody who will. In the event that you need an accomplice, they'll become one or discover one. This ability to make a special effort to furnish you with initiative and support dismantles them near you—into your Inner Circle. While they additionally may be in your Support or Service Circle due to their callings, it's their dynamic job in your own investing achievement that makes them extraordinary. For instance, they might be contractual workers, property supervisors, or land specialists, however at this point, for you, they're that and that's just the beginning. They are your guides, advisors, and accomplices, and you will contact them at any rate once per month.

4.2.2 Your Support Circle

Your Support Circle is made out of the key guardian individuals in your land investment life. As trustees, they are continually paying special mind to your best advantage. They are the experts you depend on to educate you on both the subtleties with respect to explicit exchanges and the general population you should finish them. On the off chance that needs be, they will even contract and deal with a portion of those connections for you. They are the land operators, banks, bookkeepers, and other people who are gotten on each open door in a significant manner and are vital to pretty much every exchange somehow or another. These are your exchange guides and directors—your "transactioneers."

Think about your Support Circle as investment organization officials who are not on the finance. They can deal with any of the exchange pieces for you and, if need be, can deal with every one of them. For instance, your contractual worker may flee a greens keeper to you or contract one for you. Your land operator may interface you with a property director or give one as an administration. It is the organizations they are in that will decide their essential job in the exchange. Your Support Circle frames the establishment of the expert group you depend on, and you contact these individuals on each exchange.

4.2.3 Your Service Circle

Your Service Circle is made out of particular self-employed entities and specialists. These specialist organizations will perform explicit capacities for a specific property or exchange. They are the examiners, circuit repairmen, painters, and others you may require contingent upon the circumstance. Yet, their extension is constrained. What they contact in an exchange more often than not is restricted to what they explicitly do or the extraordinary administration they give. You will by and by direct them in the work they do, or your help group will oversee them. At last, the subtleties of the exchange will direct which administration experts you will require. These are the troopers on the bleeding edge of your riches building, and you can't prevail without them. They are the talented experts who physically contact the exchange and the investment. Keep in mind: What they do, how well they do it, how quick they do it, and what they charge for doing it can represent the deciding moment any arrangement. Your Service Circle gives the particular work you requirement for a specific circumstance, and you will contact these individuals at whatever point their administrations are required.

4.2.4 Operating your Work Network

One of the greatest difficulties for most investors is realizing when to request help. Most hold up until they really need it and thus end up taking the assistance they can get as opposed to getting the assistance they need. This is the thing that isolates moguls from every other person. Moguls don't pause. Indeed, they comprehend this issue so well that they make getting into associations with the perfect individuals before they need them their main need. Working with this Network is the simple part; finding the perfect individuals and building it are not all that simple. It isn't so much that it's in reality hard—it's that it will require investment. On the off chance that you expect to be fruitful, truth be told, effective people will fit the bill to be in your Work Network. That is the reason it requires investment. You should turn over a great deal of stones to discover your Network treasures. As trying as this may appear, it isn't that hard to do. It's essentially an issue of time on the assignment. To manufacture a quality Work Network, you should invest the energy important to achieve it.

4.2.5 Work Network Maintenance

On the other hand, when you have somebody in one of your circles, you're a long way from done. You would prefer only not to construct a Work Network—you need to keep up it for the remainder of your investing life. Keeping up your Network is tied in with structure strong connections and a notoriety people can trust. Again and again in our examination, we heard the expression "relationship and notoriety equivalent arrangements," to the point where we understood we were hearing a mantra. We were catching wind of the two

Rs of systems administration: Relationship and Reputation. Connections are worked by correspondence, and Reputations are worked by reputation. The straightforward one-two-three arrangement for keeping up strong connections goes this way: Call them—Mail them—See Them. Each progression speaks to a one of a kind method to contact your Work Network, or what we some of the time allude to in lead age as a "contact."

In the first place, consider them consistently. Discover how they are getting along, share how you're doing, and talk about land investing. Only a few calls multi day will enable you to contact for all intents and purposes everybody in your Work Network each month. Second, mail them something of intrigue and esteem each month. Make a mailing rundown of your Work Network individuals in your contact database and send them a news story, an intriguing story, or counsel on land investing. Incorporate a transcribed note. One mailing a month is all it will take.

Third, for the general population in your Inner Circle, see them consistently and complete one extra thing: Pay them an individual visit every month. Breakfast, lunch, supper, or only some espresso will do. You will likely reveal to them what you're doing, audit your Net worth Worksheet with them, and request their recommendation and direction. You most likely will have close to three to five genuine coaches, so this involves just a couple of gatherings seven days. Keeping up your Work Network comes down to three straightforward inquiries you pose to yourself: Who am I calling today? Who am I seeing this week? Who am I mailing to this month? That is everything necessary. Time

wraps up.

4.2.6 Work Network Engagement

Notoriety will take somewhat longer to fabricate. It is the kind of person you are and a big motivator for you in their psyches and it requires some investment and cooperation for that to turn out to be clear. That implies you should connect with your Network all the time and in the correct manner. Here are the five things you should do after some time to build up a reputation that will cause the general population in your Work Network to regard and confide in you. We consider them the Five Rules of Engagement.

The First Rule of Engagement is to do bargains. You should be a player in the land investment amusement. Search for land openings, make offers, and do bargains. Else, you're not by any stretch of the imagination an investor. You're not taking the guidance you're being given, and you're not contracting your Network. At the end of the day, you could be squandering their time.

The Second Rule of Engagement is to keep your statement. Continuously state what you mean and mean what you state. Walk your discussion. You need to wind up known as somebody who is solid, somebody individuals can trust. Try not to miss arrangements or appear late. Satisfy your commitments. It's tied in with being the place you state you'll be and doing what you state you'll do.

The Third Rule of Engagement isn't to speak awful about anybody. This is tied in with keeping your negative considerations about others to yourself. Individuals will trust that in the event that you talk about others to them, you'll talk about them to other people. Nobody confides in a tattle.

The Fourth Rule of Engagement isn't to bamboozle anybody. Give individuals the time you guaranteed and the cash you consented to pay. Attempting to escape giving individuals the consideration or cash they merit is the quickest path there is to destroy your notoriety.

The Fifth Rule of Engagement is to elude business to your Work Network. Make a special effort to get others to utilize your Work Network. The speediest method to indicate you trust and care about individuals is to prescribe them to other people. When you elude individuals from your system to other people, you're constructing their organizations and sending them a groundbreaking message.

You will connect with the various circles of your Network at various occasions. You're Inner Circle—your guides, advisors, and accomplices—represent your most esteemed working connections. You'll see these individuals consistently whether you have progressing work or not. These are the people who help set your vision, your objectives, and your techniques for accomplishing them.

Those in your Support Circle are called vigorously with pretty much every exchange. These experts will give priceless administration and guidance throughout working out an arrangement. Your Service Circle is locked in on an "as-required" premise. Each exchange will be extraordinary and will manage the certified masters you'll require. Working with these people will harden your notoriety and after some time extend these connections. Your Work Network can move toward becoming what you need it to progress toward becoming and at last mirror your vision for your life. On the off chance that you have aspiration and objectives, it will reflect them. On the off chance that you don't, it will mirror that. To accomplish your own money related dreams you should encircle yourself with guides, bolster consultants, and specialist organizations that coordinate your monetary dreams.

4.3 The Lead Generation Model

Presumably the most widely recognized inquiry on the tip of each new investor's tongue is "Since I'm prepared to contribute, how would I discover extraordinary investment properties?" The Lead Generation Model of the Real Estate Investor responds to that question. Without leads—planned properties that resemble extraordinary chances—your investment plan can't be cultivated. To be effective, you need drives—bunch of them; in actuality the more, the better. With more leads you get more chances, and with more open doors you get the chance to pick the absolute best among them. This is the thing that tycoons do. They get the most leads and accordingly get the best properties. You could state its amount of chances first and nature of picks second. This is the reason tycoons pay attention to lead age and take it enormous. They realize that discovering incredible investment properties are a numbers diversion and that "the quality is in the amount." Finding investment properties isn't simple, yet it isn't confused either. It's tied in with recognizing what you're searching for and searching for it. Regularly, investors aren't clear enough about what they need to discover and along these lines aren't sure how to discover it. Or on the other hand more awful, this absence of lucidity drives them to discover the wrong property and error it for the correct one. This is the place the Lead Generation Model of the Real Estate Investor comes in. It crosses over any barrier between your investment objectives and the investment properties that will enable you to accomplish them. It not exclusively will educate your property look yet in addition control it. Many individuals confound doing the wrong thing with misfortune. The Lead Generation Model tells you the best way to prospect and market for investment leads and is one of the primary ways you can remove karma from the investment amusement.

Your Lead Generation Model is driven by your Criteria—the financial and physical subtleties of a property that would best meet you're investing objectives. As Millionaire Real Estate Investor George Meidoff put it, "Your Criteria structure the operational base from which you settle on the entirety of your investment choices."

Your Criteria furnish you with as exact an image as conceivable of your optimal investment property, and the more clear that image is, the better the chances are that you'll remember it when you see it. Knowing precisely what you're searching for encourages you filter through huge quantities of leads proficiently and has the additional advantage of helping you make offers rapidly and certainly once you discover a match. Clear Criteria fill in as a needed blurb, a missing property report you flow through your prospecting and advertising endeavors. The nature of your Criteria and how unmistakably you impart them eventually can decide the nature of the leads you get from your lead age endeavors. It will pay extraordinary profits to construct your Criteria cautiously in the first place and reexamine them after some time as experience manages.

Basically, on the other hand, that you don't have a clue what you're searching for, in what manner will you realize when you've discovered it? Possibly progressively significant, in what capacity will somebody help you discover it? It's anything but difficult to state you're searching for underestimated properties that will acknowledge and income, yet what does that truly mean? It's the contrast between saying you're searching for an "investment property" and saying you're searching for a "well-kept three-room, two-washroom single-story block house with a two-vehicle carport that was worked over the most recent 10 years and that can be purchased underneath market esteem." If you will put resources into land, you should be clear about what you need to put resources into—that are you're Criteria. Having no Criteria drives you anyplace and all over the place however at last abandons you no place. Having Criteria drives you where you need to go. Having explicit Criteria enables you to limit your hunt and create ability about the sorts of property you need to put resources into. Land Investors have obviously characterized Criteria. Indeed, they have two arrangements of Criteria: what they will consider and what they will purchase. The first is to some degree general, and the second is unmistakable.

The extraordinary thing about your Criteria for what you'll consider is that you can utilize them to limit your pursuit in two distinct ways. You can put them at the front end of your lead age, in this manner getting less yet better leads, or put them at the back end and consequently get more leads yet of less quality. Whichever way will work, so investigation to see which works best for you. In the primary example you're "what you'll consider" Criteria fill in as your channel toward the front, and in the second those Criteria fill in as your channel toward the back.

You will discover that working with suspects rather than prospects costs time and cash and generally isn't gainful. Along these lines, your lead age at last should incorporate a capability and end process, and that is the thing that you're "what you'll purchase" Criteria will accomplish for you: channel and kill the suspects and recognize and qualify the prospects. The reason you would once in a while to lead age with your "what I'll purchase" Criteria is that your inquiry could be narrow to the point that you'd pass up on some incredible chances. That is the reason you begin with the general declaration "I purchase houses" and after that limited it down with "I purchase houses that meet my particular Criteria." This arranging procedure is a standout amongst the most ideal approaches to create mastery in the sorts of properties you've focused on. Each property you see, each speculate you wipe out, each prospect you research, and each arrangement you eventually make builds your insight and refines your Criteria. Consider it "hands on preparing." You may even say, "The arrangement is in the subtleties." There are seven noteworthy classes you should settle on choices going to characterize your investment property Criteria: Location, Type, Economic, Condition, Construction, Features, and Amenities. The initial three—Location, Type, and Economic—are primary and are the most significant. We should investigate those three.

4.3.1 Location

The main territory where Real Estate Investors tight their hunt is area. Picking a geographic zone not just keeps the procedure reasonable and moderate; it additionally enables you to turn into a specialist rapidly. It's about core interest. It's tied in with represent considerable authority in an area, subdivision, or neighborhood until you have an unmistakable comprehension of the considerable number of elements that decide nearby property estimations and rental rates. Those qualities and rates are at last near. On the off chance that a zone comprises basically of single-family block homes with three rooms and two showers, it's imperative to know whether a house with two rooms and one shower with siding will in general sell or lease for less. This sort of near valuing runs right from significant highlights, for example, rooms, restrooms, and area to littler subtleties, for example, vaulted roofs and attractive arranging. Picking a territory encourages you ace this data all the more rapidly so you can settle on educated choices about the properties you find there.

The physical area might be a standout amongst the most significant factors in the estimation of a home. Essentially, the normal home in an extraordinary neighborhood quite often directions a more expensive rate than completes an indistinguishable home in a less alluring region. "Area, area, area" is the most established adage in the land book, yet it stays legitimate. Absolutely always remember it or become weary of saying it, since area is the one thing about any property that is difficult to copy; area is the thing that gives each bit of land its actual uniqueness.

4.3.2 Type

The second fundamental region of Criteria is property type. Is it true that you are searching for single family homes or multifamily properties, urban or rural, resort or farm, new development or resale, parts or land? Since we've concentrated on investing in private land—properties individuals live in—we should investigate the single-family and multifamily properties. You can obtain houses, townhouses, and lofts exclusively or get them in clusters by acquiring duplexes, triplexes, four-plexes, and much bigger condominium and high rises. The standard way of thinking is that solitary family homes offer the most solid interest and thankfulness while multifamily properties offer the best open doors for income. Superficially this plays out. In many markets, most of purchasers need to possess a home, thus this interest will in general keep costs moving upward after some time. Likewise, all around, the market for single-family homes is set by non-investors. These people are purchasing a home, and passionate elements play into their eagerness to purchase at a specific cost. Multifamily properties, interestingly, are purchased and sold to a great extent by investors, and this implies that their costs are resolved impartially by the estimation of the rents they speak to.

4.3.3 Economic

Essentially, you can't construct your Economic Criteria except if you have a firm thought of what properties are extremely worth. Any effective investor will reveal to you that it pays to realize property estimations and rental rates. All things considered, it's fundamental. You need to comprehend current market costs for property deals and current market rental rates to realize what your Economic Criteria ought to be. As a rule, it's ideal to be the place the biggest market is, and as a rule, most of tenants and purchasers will be in the normal valued properties. In this market section bigger quantities of tenants and purchasers can build request and drive appreciation. You're playing the midpoints to have the best chances for progress.

With your area and property type close by, invest some energy becoming more acquainted with property estimations and rental rates. You need to start perusing paper and Internet postings and taking notes. On the other hand, that you drive or stroll through your objective zone, put aside time to drop in on open houses and assess rentals.

4.4 The Acquisition Model

So far you've contributed your time; presently it's an ideal opportunity to contribute your cash. You're at the land investor's decision time, where dreams work out as expected or not, where money related riches is made or lost. It's an ideal opportunity to profit. How do tycoons profit? It's straightforward: They make their cash going in. By following the Acquisition Model and purchasing right, they for all intents and purposes ensure the achievement of their investments. That is the thing that you need to do: You need to figure out how to pursue the Acquisition Model of the Real Estate Investor. In the event that you can buy property with enough benefit worked in, you will have guaranteed, at the time you purchase, that your investments will profit. This is significant in light of the fact that once you start to make land acquisitions, your presentation will be recorded for all time and always—no replays or second chances. In the event that you adhere to the Acquisition Model, you won't require any.

By sharing the well-earned intelligence and genuine encounters of our Real Estate Investors, we have been both setting up your psyche and advising your activities to get your investment plans propelled. You currently comprehend the Path of Money, you've planned with the goal that you have cash to contribute, and you've set up your Personal Balance Sheet so you can keep tabs on your development. You realize how land investing can expand your total assets through value development and income development. You've started to fabricate your

Work Network with the goal that you will have the group you have to tutor you, bolster you, and administration your investments. You've built up your Criteria, and you're lead-producing for it. Presently you have leads, imminent chances to put resources into, and you should begin deciding. The choices you make and the moves you make in these basic minutes can profoundly affect your money related riches building.

4.4.1 Cash Flow and Equity

In land investing there are just two central securing methodologies: purchase for money and purchase for income and value development. There are numerous specializations and varieties inside every one of these fundamental procedures, and they frequently are alluded to by different names, for example, optioning, accepting, rehabbing, long haul investing, speedy turn investing, wholesaling, wrapping, rent optioning, and fixing and flipping. In any case, each one of those names simply entangles the image.

Regardless of what you call them, these systems come down to one straightforward truth—investors contribute for Cash or contribute for Cash Flow and Equity. One is a money building methodology, and the other is a riches building one. You should simply choose which of these two techniques you need or need to utilize and after that pursue the model for it.

For certain investors, as a result of their objectives or current conditions, money is above all else. On the off chance that you need money, you have four fundamental alternatives for amassing it: Find and Refer, Control and Assign, Buy and Sell, and Buy, Improve, and Sell. On the other hand, that you are searching for money and would prefer not to contribute any cash or even compose an agreement, you can achieve that through Find and Refer. You can turn into a scout. As a scout, you search out wise investment openings and afterward convey them to investors who are prepared and willing to secure those properties. By and large, they will pay you a "discoverer's expense" if the open doors are great and they would not have found them generally. This is likely the quickest method to acquire money and by a wide margin the choice you can do the large portion of regarding numbers. The downside is that the cash paid per exchange is the least among the four choices.

The second quickest alternative to procure money is Control and Assign. This implies you gain an alternative or an assignable contract on an investment property and afterward discover another person to obtain it. Since you control the property, you have arrangement control. This technique has a little preferable edge over Find and Refer, yet the volume potential is somewhat less.

At last the main role of the four money building systems is to create quick money, salary which can be utilized as earned pay or set back into play along the Path of Money. A large number of the investors we chatted with at some time utilized every one of these techniques to dispatch their land investing vocations. When they did them right, which they will caution you isn't as simple as it regularly is described, they had the option to develop some money reserve funds, which they could use as initial installments on pay properties. They were taking money and reinvesting it for income and value: long haul budgetary riches building.

4.4.2 Buying and Selling Terms

In the Buy and Sell system you are searching for a certain something—money. The objective is to guarantee a net benefit result inside weeks or at most months by purchasing a property and after that pivoting and offering it. Despite the fact that this technique more often than not has the greatest settlements, it accompanies one major test: You should know your numbers, bunches of them. What's more, on the off chance that you are going to Buy, Improve, and Sell, there are considerably more numbers you have to know and get it. Your numbers must be exact going in. You are making a progression of expectations, all of which need to turn out basically as figure for the arrangement to be a triumph. You should be correct or you better have worked in a genuine edge for blunder.

The value a property may sell for versus the value it will 'rapidly' sell for can be the distinction in controlling your conveying costs and, in particular, making a precise introductory estimation about anticipated benefits. The normal benefits build up the underlying offer cost on the house. In this way, when estimating your sell cost doesn't simply consider the after fix esteem, consider likewise the 'quick' after fix esteem."

A considerable lot of the homes focused by Buy and Sell investors are frequently at the high low end or lower center market. This implies you're not continually pitching to purchasers with heaps of money for shutting and impeccable credit. The extraordinary offer you acknowledge may fall through in view of financing or credit issues. This could mean beginning once again, and that implies time.

Starting here on, as you make extra enhancements, you will expand the market estimation of the property. You are in the prime improvement zone. In any case, know that this expansion in esteem has a reasonable point of confinement: what the market will bear. From here on any extra investment in enhancements won't include much, assuming any, showcase incentive to the property. You have achieved the purpose of Maximum Return on Investment. It is presently time to maintain a strategic distance from over-improving the property and put it on the resale advertise quick, money in on your overall revenue, and proceed onward to the following investment.

Knowing which upgrades, at what cost, will bring the Maximum Return is a definitive expertise in this diversion. It's the round of getting the most elevated come back from minimal investment in enhancements. Investors with development experience and those with do-it-without anyone else's help aptitudes and a strong learning of fix work can do well with Buy, Improve, and Sell. In addition to the fact that they enter the diversion with an educated thought regarding the expenses and time expected to do regular fixes, however they are likewise fit for doing a significant number of those fixes themselves. This perspiration value enables them to trade their time and work for diminished costs and bigger overall revenues. A great many people, in any case, will require the counsel of an accomplished temporary worker and the assistance of a strong group of fix and renovating experts to advance this system.

This is a basic point in the Buy and Hold procurement model. In the event that the property does not create income with the numbers you have, you should bring down your offer suitably or look for unique financing. The correct terms on your advance can regularly have a critical effect. The investors we conversed with were incredibly inventive in their financing arrangements. They saw how to exploit variable-rate and movable rate customary home loans to get quick income on the arrangement.

CHAPTER 5: HOW TO RAISE FINANCING AND CAPITAL

5.1 Recognizing Capital Sources

For some individuals, the issue with land investing is that they come up short on the entrance to money for the initial installment. The familiar aphorism that "it takes cash to profit" is commonly valid as far as we can tell. Most land investing books make one of two presumptions. Some expect that you have a lot of cash and simply need to make sense of how to purchase, increase the value of a property, and afterward sell. Obviously, that should were valid, however not every person is flush with money. The other regular supposition that will be that you have no cash and should fall back on scouring the land showcase looking for venders so edgy to sell that they or their banks don't require any up front installment. We expect not one or the other. So how would you begin in land in the event that you would prefer not to claim bothered properties in the most noticeably awful neighborhoods, and you don't have a six-figure balance in your financial balance to pay as much as possible in the best neighborhoods? You gather all the tolerance you can and grasp a long haul vision. You don't need to be rich or have incredible funds to start making appealing land investments. In this book, we present a wide scope of investment choices, so there's something for all intents and purposes everybody's financial limit and individual circumstance. Our technique for structure land riches after some time is to make investment restores that are manageable and give liberal profits for your investments. More often than not, land investors make an initial installment and get most of the cash expected to finish a buy. That is the customary method to buy land investment properties and will be the best technique for you over the long haul (as it has been for us).

So as to fit the bill for the most alluring financing, moneylenders normally necessitate that your initial installment be in any event 20 percent of the property's price tag. The best investment property advances at times expect 25 to 30 percent down for the most positive terms. Loan specialists will in general be progressively traditionalist and require bigger up front installments amid times of falling land costs, for example, most territories experienced in the late 2000s. For most private investment properties, for example, single-family homes, connected lodging, for example, condominiums and townhomes, and little loft structures of up to four units, you can gain admittance to the best financing terms by making in any event a 20 to 25 percent up front installment. You might almost certainly make littler up front installments (as low as 10 percent or less), yet you'll pay a lot higher financing costs and credit charges, including private home loan protection.

Deciding how a lot of money you have to close on a buy is generally a component of the arranged price tag, including every single shutting cost and charges. Assume you're hoping to get some unassuming private lodging for $100,000. For a 25 percent up front installment you need $25,000, and including another 5 percent for shutting costs brings you to $30,000. On the off chance that you have your heart set on purchasing a property that costs three fold the amount

($300,000 sticker value); you have to significantly increase these sums to a sum of about $90,000 for the best financing choices. Best land investors that we know, including us, began building their land investment portfolio as it was done in the good 'old days — through setting aside some cash and after that steadily purchasing properties throughout the years. Numerous individuals experience issues setting aside some cash since they don't have a clue how to or are basically reluctant to confine their spending. Simple access to customer obligation (through charge cards and vehicle credits) makes immense snags to sparing more and spending less. Investing in land requires restraint, penance, and order. Like most beneficial things throughout everyday life, you should be patient and plan ahead to have the option to put resources into land. Strong training is the way to more noteworthy money related rewards and prompts the majority of the extraordinary objectives we talk about here. Instruction is key for your picked calling as well as for land investing. Consider getting a land permit or figure out how to be an appraiser or property chief — abilities that help you with your property investing as well as may enable you to take on low maintenance work to enhance your salary.

Setting aside extra cash from your month to month profit will likely be the establishment for your land investing program. Be that as it may, you may approach other budgetary assets for up front installments. Before we bounce into these, we offer a well-disposed little update: Monitor the amount of your general investment portfolio you place into land and how expanded and proper your possessions are given your general objectives. A few businesses enable you to get against your retirement account balance, under the condition that you reimburse the credit inside a set number of years. Subject to qualification necessities, first-time homebuyers can make punishment free withdrawals of up to $10,000 from IRA accounts.

Most land investors that we know started assembling their land portfolio after they purchased their very own home. Moderately taking advantage of your home's value might be a decent up front installment hotspot for your property investments. You can for the most part get contract cash at a lower financing cost on your home than you can on investment property. The littler the hazard to the loan specialist, the lower its required return, and in this way, the better rates for you as the borrower. Loan specialists see investment property as a higher hazard suggestion and in light of current circumstances: They realize that when accounts go downhill and the going gets extremely intense, individuals pay their home loan to abstain from losing the rooftop over their heads before they pay obligations on a rentable house. Except if your present home loan was secured at lower rates than are accessible today, we for the most part prescribe renegotiating the principal trust deed advance and opening up value that way as opposed to taking out a home value advance or credit extension.

5.2 Property Purchases Financing

We know property investors who burned through handfuls to several hours finding the best areas and properties possibly to have their arrangements unwind when they were unfit to pick up endorsement for required financing. You can't play in the event that you can't pay. In spite of the fact that you can discover a huge number of various kinds of home loans, just two noteworthy classifications of home loans exist: fixed financing cost and customizable rate. In fact talking, a few home loans join components of both — they may stay fixed for various years and afterward have a variable financing cost after that.

For reasons for making future appraisals of your property's income, fixed rate contracts offer you assurance and some genuine feelings of serenity since you know unequivocally the extent of your home loan installment one month from now, one year from now, and a long time from now. You can begin paying your home loan with a generally low starting financing cost contrasted and fixed-rate credits. Given the financial matters of a commonplace investment property buy, ARMs better empower an investor to accomplish a positive income in the early long stretches of property possession.

The diverse lists utilized on ARMs fluctuate predominantly in how quickly they react to changes in loan fees. On the off chance that you select a movable rate contract attached to one of the quicker moving records, you go out on a limb on to a greater degree a hazard that the following change may reflect financing cost increments. When you go out on a limb on a greater amount of the hazard that rates may expand, moneylenders cut you some breathing room in different ways, for example, through lower tops, lower edges or lower focuses.

After the underlying financing cost closes the loan cost on an ARM changes dependent on the advance equation. Normally, ARM financing costs change each 6 or a year, yet some alter each month. Ahead of time of every alteration, the moneylender sends you a notice revealing to you your new rate. Make certain to check these notifications in light of the fact that on uncommon events, banks commit errors.

Practically all ARMs accompany a rate top, which constrains the most extreme rate change (up or down) permitted at every modification. This breaking point is normally alluded to as the alteration top. On most credits that modify at regular intervals, the change top is 1 percent; the loan cost charged on the home loan can climb or down close to one rate point in an alteration period.

As you make contract installments after some time, the advance parity regardless you owe is bit by bit diminished or amortized. Negative amortization is the invert of this procedure. It happens when the month to month advance installments are not exactly the measure of intrigue that is accumulating amid that time. A few ARMs permit negative amortization. In what capacity can your extraordinary credit balance develop when you keep on making contract installments? This marvel happens when your home loan installment is short of what it should be.

A few advances to the expansion of your regularly scheduled installment sum however don't top the financing cost. Along these lines, the extent of your home loan installment may not mirror all the intrigue that you right now owe on your credit. Along these lines, instead of paying the intrigue that you owe and satisfying a portion of your advance equalization (or chief) consistently, you end up satisfying a few, yet not all, of the intrigue that you owe. Subsequently, banks include the additional, unpaid premium that despite everything you owe to your exceptional obligation.

Negative amortization is like paying just the base installment that your Visa bill requires. You keep on racking up money charges on the unpaid equalization as long as you just make the misleadingly low installment. Taking a home loan with negative amortization invalidates the general purpose of obtaining a sum that accommodates your by and large money related objectives.

Maintain a strategic distance from ARMs with negative amortization. The best way to know whether an advance incorporates negative amortization is to ask unequivocally. A few loan specialists and home loan representatives aren't pending about letting you know. In the event that you experience difficulty discovering banks that will manage your budgetary circumstance, ensure that you're particularly cautious — you discover negative amortization all the more much of the time on credits that loan specialists think about dangerous, which ought to be taken as a sign that perhaps you're exceeding for a property that isn't a perfect investment. You're likely just to consider such a home loan on the grounds that your income won't enable you to have a completely amortized advance. In this manner you would need to accomplish huge thankfulness in the property to cover this negative income in addition to your ideal rate of return all together for this investment to bode well.

5.3 Best Mortgage Financing

Picking between a fixed-rate or flexible rate credit is a significant choice in the land investment process. Consider the points of interest and disservices of each home loan type and choose what's best for your circumstance before going out to renegotiate or buy land. What amount of hazard would you be able to deal with concerning the extent of your property's month to month contract installment? In the event that you can go for broke that accompany an ARM, you have a superior shot of setting aside extra cash and boosting your property's income with a movable rate as opposed to a fixed-rate advance. Your loan fee begins lower and stays lower with an ARM, if the general dimension of financing costs remains unaltered. Regardless of whether rates go up, they'll likely return over the life of your credit. On the off chance that you can stay with your ARM for better and for more awful, you should outpace the competition over the long haul.

ARMs bode well on the off chance that you get short of what you're equipped for. On the off chance that your pay (and material investment property income) essentially surpasses your spending, you may feel less nervousness about the fluctuating financing cost on an ARM. On the off chance that you do pick a flexible advance, you may feel all the more monetarily safe in the event that you have a weighty budgetary pad (in any event a half years to as much as a year of costs saved) that you can get to if rates go up. A few people take ARMs when they can't generally bear the cost of them. At the point when rates rise, property proprietors who can't bear the cost of higher installments face a money related emergency. On the off chance that you don't have crisis investment funds that you can take advantage of to make the higher installments, how might you bear the cost of the regularly scheduled installments and different costs of your property?

Sparing enthusiasm on most ARMs is typically an assurance in the initial a few years. A movable rate contract begins at a lower financing cost than a fixed one. Be that as it may, if rates rise, you can finish up reimbursing the investment funds that you accomplish in the early long stretches of the home loan.

In the event that you aren't going to keep your home loan for more than five to seven years, you pay more enthusiasm to convey a fixed-rate contract. A home loan bank goes for broke in focusing on a fixed-financing cost for 15 to 30 years. Loan specialists don't have the foggiest idea what may occur in the interceding years, so they charge you a premium in the event that financing costs move fundamentally higher in future years. You may likewise think about a cross breed advance, which consolidates highlights of fixed-and customizable rate contracts. For instance, the underlying rate may hold steady for three, five, seven, or ten years and afterward change once per year or like clockwork from that point. Such credits may bode well for you on the off chance that you anticipate a high likelihood of keeping your advance seven to ten years or less however need some security in your future regularly scheduled installments. The more drawn out the underlying rate stays secured in, the higher the financing cost. Try not to mistake these advances for the regularly unadvisable inflatable home loan.

Most home loan banks offer you the choice of 15-year or 30-year contracts. You can likewise discover 10-year, 20-year, and 40-year alternatives, however they're bizarre. A few loan specialists are notwithstanding enabling you to choose tweaked or other length amortization terms that enable you to customize the quantity of long stretches of your home loan. Customizing your home loan may bode well on the off chance that you have a particular objective as a main priority, for example, finishing your home loan installments before handling school educational cost bills or a retirement date. So how would you choose whether a shorter-or longer-term contract is best for your investment property buy?

To bear the cost of the regularly scheduled installments and have a positive income, numerous investment property purchasers need to spread their home loan credit installments over a more drawn out timeframe, and a 30-year contract is the best approach to do it. A 15-year contract has higher regularly scheduled installments since you pay it off faster. At a fixed rate contract loan cost of 7 percent, for instance, a 15-year contract accompanies installments that are around 35 percent higher than those for a 30-year contract.

A home value advance may give a moderately minimal effort wellspring of assets for an investment property buy, particularly in case you're looking for cash for only a couple of years. You can renegotiate your first home loan and haul money out for an investment property buy, however we don't prompt doing that if your first home loan is at a lower financing cost than you can acquire on a renegotiate. Home value advances for the most part have higher financing costs than equivalent first home loans since they're less secure to a moneylender. The reason: if you default on the main home loan or seek financial protection assurance, the principal contract bank gets first case on your home.

Few out of every odd merchant needs or even needs to get all money as installment for his property, so you might almost certainly money part or even the majority of an investment property buy because of the property dealer's financing. The utilization of dealer financing is the foundation of most no-cash down techniques.

Dealer financing is an exchange wherein the vender acknowledges anything short of all money at shutting. One type of an all-money exchange to the merchant is the purchaser truly paying all money, yet regularly it's an exchange wherein the purchaser utilizes a standard mortgage (cash to buy the property from a bank other than the dealer) with the goal that the vender adequately gets all money at shutting. A few dealers are monetarily sufficiently wealthy that they needn't bother with the majority of the business continues promptly for their next buy or are purchasing a property for less cash — or possibly not purchasing a substitution property by any means — and want to get installments after some time. They might search for the installments to supplant their pay in retirement or they may want to get the assets after some time so they can lessen their assessable salary.

CHAPTER 6: PROPERTIES IDENTIFICATION AND EVALUATION

6.1 Value of Location

As the outstanding land saying goes, "The three most significant components to accomplishment in land are area, area, and area!" There is a solid relationship between the area of your land investments and your money related achievement. What's more, we solidly concur that the area of your land investment is basic in deciding your prosperity as a land investor.

Just owning land isn't the way to achievement in land investing; securing and owning the correct land at the correct cost is the way to manufacture riches! As you gain involvement in land, you'll build up your very own procedure, yet to make any methodology succeed, you have to get your work done and steadily and decently assess both the positive and negative parts of your proposed land investment. That is the place we come in.

Although essentially everybody lives in a zone with open doors for land investing, not every person lives in a zone where the prospects are useful for land when all is said in done. That is the reason it's imperative to expand your geographic investment skyline as long as you don't bargain your capacity to successfully oversee and control your property.

Regardless of whether you choose to put resources into land in your own district, despite everything you have to do huge amounts of research to choose where and what to purchase — critical choices with long haul outcomes. In the pages that pursue, we disclose what to search for in an area, a network, and even an area before you settle on that investment choice. Remember, however, that you can spend a mind-blowing remainder searching for the ideal land investment, never discover it, never contribute, and pass up bunches of chances, benefit, and even fun.

So you're searching for properties that enable you to make physical as well as monetary upgrades that will at last lower the normal top rate to a future investor, which is basically bringing down the required rate of return since you have gone for broke out a great part of the hazard. You need to purchase when you discover that the property has a solid probability of creating future increments in NOI and income. So you should search for properties where your investigation demonstrates that the pay for the property can be expanded or the costs decreased.

As you search for your next investment property, numerous merchants, and particularly their land intermediaries, will guarantee you that the flow rents are actually excessively low, and that there is huge upside in the property to be tapped essentially by purchasing the property and raising the rents. On the other hand, that it was just that simple, at that point for what reason wouldn't the present proprietor raise the lease and after that sell the property at a greater expense?

In any case, in the event that you completely inquire about the market, you'll realize how to recognize certain hints that show whether a property truly has rents that are underneath market. Properties without any opening and a holding up rundown are prime competitors. Other indications are properties that have low turnover and after that have various candidates for those uncommon opportunities.

A few proprietors really advertise their land investment properties at an underneath market cost. These are roused venders, most likely with an assortment of individual explanations behind their need to sell more rapidly and inexpensively than they would on the off chance that they had additional time and tolerance. Wellbeing reasons, family disintegrations, money related issues, etc. are for the most part likely reasons that a merchant will consent to a brisk deal at an underneath market cost.

On the other hand, a few dealers don't accomplish the operation esteem in the market for different reasons. For instance, a few proprietors loathe the entire procedure of selling their investment properties so much that they purposely undervalue the property to guarantee a fast and clean exchange and hold the capacity to dismiss any possibilities that a purchaser would commonly require in a market bargain. The end of bothering and wheeling and dealing is fundamental to these venders; they simply need to complete the deal, so they're willing to give the purchaser such a decent arrangement, that the purchaser takes the property basically in its present condition.

A straightforward case of how to expand the estimation of a structure is to locate a private investment property in an extreme interest zone where every single rental rate is the equivalent for comparative floor plans. As a general rule, the rents ought to mirror the way that, state, not every one of the two-room units have a similar area benefits. For instance, a unit sitting above the pool is regularly more attractive than a unit on the primary road or units on the upper floors are in more prominent interest, so raising the rents for the more alluring units builds rental pay.

In spite of the fact that we encourage you to think neighborhood, any choice about where to contribute should begin with an assessment of the generally speaking monetary suitability and patterns of the encompassing district. In the event that the locale isn't monetarily stable, the probability for effective land investments inside that region is lessened. See how to assess significant financial information with the goal that you can put resources into the territories that are balanced for development. Assembling and breaking down the applicable financial information has never been simpler, on account of the Internet. The most significant information for populace development, work development, and financial patterns is accessible on the web, and there are various elements following this data. From the government, to state and neighborhood governments, to colleges and business gatherings, data on provincial monetary patterns is promptly accessible.

6.2 Leases and Property Valuation

A rent is an authoritative commitment between a lessor (landowner) and a renter (occupant) to exchange the privilege to selective belonging and utilization of certain genuine property for a characterized timespan for a concurred thought (cash). A verbal rent can be enforceable, yet it's greatly improved to have a composed rent that characterizes the rights and duties of the landowner and the occupant. Owning an investment property with alluring and all around kept up structures may give you a feeling of pride of possession, yet what you're truly investing in is the leases. Effective land investors realize that a great open door is to discover properties with leases that offer upside potential as higher salary as well as steadiness of occupancy.

A dealer ought to be straightforward and unveil every single material actuality about the property he's selling, yet most states don't have the equivalent composed revelation prerequisites that are commanded for private exchanges. So despite the fact that your merchant or deals operator and different individuals from your due tirelessness examination group might help you with investigating the property and looking into the books gave amid the exchange, recollect that you should be the person who thinks the most about your best advantages.

The investigation of current leases for private properties is typically genuinely clear, yet that doesn't mean you shouldn't get your work done! Audit every single private rent to ensure that no shrouded shocks are anticipating you, for example, future free lease, breaking points to lease increments, or guarantees of new floor covering or other costly overhauls. Some subtle merchants of private properties realize that a few purchasers don't completely audit each rent, so they load the leases with future lease concessions in return for higher leases in advance, which they use to own the property's money related expressions look progressively alluring. Make certain that you decide the net compelling rent and base your idea for a property on those numbers. An obvious above-showcase rent isn't generally above market in case you're giving without end free lease or promising to supplant the rug upon rent reestablishment. Business leases are significantly more convoluted than private ones. In this way, the business land investor must have a careful comprehension of the legally binding commitments and obligations of the lessor (proprietor) and resident (occupant).

The examination of business leases is ordinarily called rent reflection. A rent theoretical is a composed outline of all the critical terms and conditions contained in the rent and is substantially more than a lease roll. In spite of the fact that a decent lease move covers the rent fundamentals — lease, area, length of rent, and reestablishment date or choices — a decent conceptual spreads other key occupant issues, for example, signage, privileges of development and constriction, and even confinements or impediments on renting to different inhabitants that offer comparable items and administrations. Have composed rent abstracts arranged for any business property you're thinking about to guarantee that you see every one of the terms.

While acquiring financing for business properties, loan specialists commonly require an affirmed or marked lease move alongside a composed rent theoretical for each occupant. In any case, in light of the fact that the pay of the property is basic to the proprietor's capacity to make the obligation administration commitments, most banks don't just depend on the purchaser's numbers however freely infer their own pay projections dependent on data they require the buyer to get from the occupants.

Realizing certain monetary standards can be helpful when trying to assess the present and future estimation of potential land investments. Esteem can likewise be influenced when certain limitations, (for example, the affiliation conditions, contracts, and confinements found in many mortgage holders affiliations) are components of utility while additionally being a piece of transferability since they keep running with the land and point of confinement the privileges of future proprietors.

These monetary standards depend on the reason that the most extreme estimation of land is accomplished when a property is being used in its most astounding and best use. Most astounding and best use is the essential idea that there is one single utilize that outcomes in the greatest gainfulness by the best and most proficient utilization of the property. The most elevated and best utilization of a particular property doesn't stay steady after some time. Zoning of a property can wipe out certain potential employments of a property at the season of assessment. On the other hand, especially for properties in the way of advancement, time can make new chances. Land investors experience another sort of significant worth — investment esteem. Despite the fact that the market esteem is the estimation of a property to a run of the mill investor, investment esteem is its incentive to a particular investor dependent on his specific necessities, for example, the expense of capital, charge rate, or individual objectives. Sometime in the not so distant future, you may end up going up against another purchaser for a prime investment property just to be astounded that she appears to pay substantially more. On the off chance that you've painstakingly investigated the property, and the dealer gave a similar data about the property to every single potential buyer, the other purchaser is likely putting together her idea with respect to the property's investment incentive to her. For instance, an investor who can't utilize the tax cuts of deterioration would pay less for a property that would create vast yearly devaluation than would an investor that has other easy revenue and can utilize the deferral of tax collection to lessen his present salary charge commitments.

6.3 Property Inspections, Due Diligence, and Closing

A land exchange for even little investment properties can be confounded, on the grounds that the purchaser and merchant have various premiums that should be genuinely spoken to. The escrow holder goes about as a nonpartisan outsider who handles the subtleties of the exchange and regularly fills in as the ref when differences create among purchaser and dealer. In certain pieces of the nation, the job of the escrow officer is substantially more restricted. Your land operator can manage you with regards to the custom and practice in your general vicinity.

The escrow officer readies the escrow directions that manage the exchange between the gatherings. The escrow directions are gotten from the particular terms found in the buy understanding and in some other composed archives commonly settled upon by both the purchaser and vender.

The escrow directions are basic. To limit shocks, cautiously audit the directions before you sign them, since that is the record that the escrow holder depends upon solely to figure out what to do in case of a question. Except if permitted in the escrow directions, the escrow officer can't roll out any improvements or react to any solicitations without a composed understanding marked by all gatherings.

Not long after the escrow directions have been marked, your title organization ought to send you a duplicate of the primer title report (or prelim). Have this critical report investigated by a lawyer except if you have a great deal of individual experience and the prelim contains moderately few demonstrated things. The primer title report shows the current legitimate proprietor of the property and any home loan liens, unpaid pay charge liens, property charge liens, judgment liens, or other recorded encumbrances against the property. It additionally demonstrates any easements, limitations, or outsider interests that limit your utilization of the property, for example, the Covenants, Conditions, and Restrictions (C, C, and Rs) ordinarily found with arranged unit advancements, network affiliations, or apartment suites.

Possibilities make a kind of alternative and are basic components that can represent the deciding moment an exchange. The buy understanding and escrow directions as a rule contain due dates — the gatherings have certain rights relating to possibilities for a restricted timeframe. For instance, the physical investigation possibility may give just ten days to make the review; after that the possibility is viewed as endorsed (or fulfilled) and the merchant has the legitimate appropriate to reject access for a physical assessment.

After the majority of the purchaser's and dealer's possibilities relating to things, for example, the financing, evaluation, books and records, and the physical investigation have been met or deferred, the escrow officer instructs the gatherings regarding the assessed shutting date for the exchange.

The formal due determination time frame (the timespan between the acknowledgment of an offer and the end of escrow or consummation of the deal), is an ideal opportunity to pose those extreme inquiries. Try not to be bashful. Converse with the occupants, the neighbors, any mortgage holder's or business affiliation, legislative organizations, and the temporary workers or providers to the property, and make certain that you recognize what you're getting. Impart routinely and work intimately with the vender and his agents, however just depend on data gave recorded as a hard copy. This timeframe might be your best or just chance to look for alterations, if significant issues have been spoken to incorrectly. After the property deal is finished, it's past the point where it is possible to request that the dealer fix the defective rooftop except if she has occupied with a purposeful exertion to conceal the genuine state of the property. Your cures may just be in court, which can be exorbitant and held just for the most genuine or costly issues.

Reasonable instances of due ingenuity incorporate gathering monetary information about the area and neighborhood, calling aggressive properties for current market rental rates and concessions, checking the precision of the money related data and leases exhibited by the vender, and leading an intensive physical assessment of the property by an authorized general temporary worker or property examiner. In spite of the fact that astute land investors lead pre-offer due tirelessness and regularly get a duplicate of an ace forma working explanation, you likely won't have a chance to survey the genuine books and records until you're formally under contract and in the due persistence time frame.

In the event that the vender discounts the security stores, you have the test of gathering stores from inhabitants as of now possessing the rental unit or suite, which is never simple. Hence, emphatically ask the vender to give you an a sound representative for everything of the security stores close by retained and have each occupant concur recorded as a hard copy to the measure of the security store exchanged amid the deal. This procedure streamlines the procedure and keeps you from recalling security stores from current inhabitants. To keep away from issues at the season of move-out, send your inhabitant a letter affirming the security store sum.

Likewise see if the vender has any stores close by with the service organization and whether you have to put a store for administration. You might most likely just handle the exchange of the store through escrow with a composed store exchange affirmation from the utility. On the off chance that a survey of the property costs shows that utility expenses are strangely high, you might need to demand looking into duplicates of the genuine recorded bills so as to decide if there was a one-time fluctuation or whether the property may profit by protection endeavors.

The state of a property legitimately influences its esteem. The judicious land investor dependably demands a careful physical review before buying an investment property regardless of whether the property is spic and span. Another investment property may look great on paper and your pre-offer due perseverance may uncover no lawful or budgetary issues or concerns. On the other hand, your investment is just in the same class as the weakest connection, and a physically vexed property is never a wise investment.

Insightful land investors really have a two-advance examination process with their underlying pre-offer stroll through of the property as a prelude to making the offer. On the off chance that the offer is made and acknowledged, the expert investigation is to recognize any arrangement executioner issues with the property or any things that warrant renegotiation.

6.4 Making an Offer

You profit in land when you buy your investment property. In the event that you purchase a well-found and physically solid property underneath market esteem and substitution cost, the property will furnish you with phenomenal returns for a long time. This is the reason shrewd arranging is so critical to being effective with your land investments.

In spite of the fact that everybody approaches consulting from their own point of view, we believe that it's essential to comprehend that the land network in many territories is really an affectionate gathering of experts who arrange. In this manner, informal referrals and notoriety for trustworthiness and respectability are basic components to your long-haul achievement. Persistence, vision, and tirelessness are likewise extraordinary excellences with regards to making the best land bargains. Hard driving, uneven exchanges may profit in the short-run, however word voyages quick.

The most significant arranging device in an investment property buy is better learning —

in case you're reluctant than do the homework important to legitimize the correct cost, you're nearly ensured to overpay for land. Your objective as an investor is to set the most extreme value that you can pay and still get a strong profit for your investment in light of the related dangers.

We don't propose that you delude anybody, yet an astounding number of current property proprietors simply don't focus on even the most fundamental freely accessible data. Nothing is corrupt or unlawful about having vision to redesign and remodel a property to accomplish its full esteem in light of the fact that your exploration with neighborhood offices demonstrates that a noteworthy new boss is moving into the region, drastically expanding interest for half-empty and tired business properties — like the one you're thinking about for procurement. You'll be amazingly fruitful in arranging extraordinary land bargains in the event that you not just know the perfect individuals and have a decent land investment group yet in addition know the significant elements that influence free market activity in the neighborhood advertise.

Possibly you're seeing neighborhood organizations developing quickly and employing bunches of new specialists. You realize that as a result of a nearby lodging deficiency, the numerous new families moving into the zone will be unfit to bear the cost of another home and should lease. That is a decent sign that rents will increment and the interest will be high for pleasant three-to four-room rental homes situated in calm parkways close to the best schools.

Obviously, you can utilize this data to appropriately arrange the buy of prime rental homes in such a market.

Or on the other hand maybe the last endorsement by the neighborhood travel locale to broaden another light rail line into and through an once-over territory of the network may truly be an impetus for positive change. So you get your work done and locate a more seasoned couple who has lost enthusiasm for their business property around there. You buy and remodel this little retail strip focus opposite the new station since you know it's an alluring area for retail inhabitants focusing on workers. Decide the present free market activity in the commercial center so you realize whether it's a purchaser's or vender's market. That doesn't mean you can't even now make some extraordinary land investments; however, you should be sensible. Purchasing in a vender's market at costs above substitution cost can be risky. Try not to considerably think of it as if your objective is a transient hang on the property. Data is the core of arranging. Convey actualities to the bartering table. Get equivalent deals information to help your cost. Again and again, investors and their specialists select number from the air when they make an offer. In the event that you were the dealer, be induced to bring down your asking cost? Indicating later and tantamount investment property deals to legitimize your offer cost fortifies your case. Once in a while do you discover a vender of investment-grade land who doesn't approach a lot of market information? However, merchants frequently don't choose the privilege properties — wanting to imaginatively utilize only those comps that accommodate the most astounding conceivable asking cost.

The time that you have to close on your buy is additionally a negotiating concession. A few merchants may require money soon and surrender different focuses on the off chance that you can close rapidly. Also, the land specialist's bonus might be debatable as well. At long last, attempt decently well to let your feelings alone for any property buy. This is more difficult than one might expect, yet do whatever it takes not to go gaga for a property. Continue looking for different properties notwithstanding when you make an offer — you might consult with an unmotivated vender.

The buy understanding is the authoritative record that traces the subtleties of the exchange for your proposed buy of the subject property. Contingent upon where you live, there are different terms for an agreement for the buy of land, for example, a business contract, an idea to buy, an agreement of procurement furthermore, deal, a sincere cash understanding, and a store receipt.

Regardless of what you call it, the buy understanding is the most significant archive in the clearance of land. It incorporates the essential information — the names of the merchants and purchasers, a depiction of the property, and the proposed financing terms — and shows the amount you pay, when you pay, the terms and conditions that must be met to close the exchange, and the conditions under which the understanding can be dropped and the purchaser's store returned. Try not to give a land operator a chance to reveal to you that your offer must be on a specific structure, in light of the fact that albeit many buy understanding structures are accessible, none are required. Which structure you use is up to you — we suggest that you utilize a buy understanding structure that is anything but difficult to peruse and get it. The more confounded the language, the almost certain it is that the gatherings get befuddled or differ on the significance of the terms of the offer.

CHAPTER 7: MYTH OF TENS

7.1 Increasing Property's Value by Ten Ways

Even though most investment properties have different wellsprings of pay, the biggest source is quite often the rents. Land investors shrewdly start with an understanding that lease builds lead to more prominent income. Notwithstanding, setting the correct lease and keeping up the ideal market level endless supply of occupants is a standout amongst the most widely recognized difficulties looked by property proprietors. Numerous investment property proprietors are hesitant to raise rents since they're worried that their great occupants may leave. This is a substantial concern, yet it shouldn't keep you from getting rents to advertise level — one of the quickest and least complex approaches to improve your income. Obviously, you ought to dependably search for savvy approaches to improve the property and ensure that your rents are aggressive and a reasonable esteem. On the other hand that your rents are now at market levels, hope to make moves up to the property to legitimize higher rents. Possibly including a blend microwave/exhaust vent unit over the stove, giving extra spaces, or introducing a deck or shade can give an improvement that legitimizes higher lease. Any upgrades that improve the nature of living or convey the property to a dimension like higher estimated properties in the region can prompt expanded market rents.

The absolute most significant factor in deciding the costs of most investment properties is turnover. In both private and business properties, inhabitant turnover is basically awful for the reality. An inhabitant moving out more likely than not implies a misfortune in rental pay, in addition to your hit with the expanded costs (promoting, occupant screening, support and fixes, and regularly capital upgrades) to make the rental unit or suite accessible to indicate imminent occupants. Marking long haul leases with qualified inhabitants, ceaselessly keeping up the property in top condition, and being receptive to the occupants can help decrease inhabitant turnover, which legitimately improves the Net Operating Income and income.

Another compelling device to lessen the loss of lease amid occupant turnover is to prelease the rental unit or inhabitant suite. In the event that you can prelease the rental to another inhabitant just a couple of days or weeks after the present occupant abandons, you drastically diminish your lost lease and increment your income. After you get an occupant's notice to clear, promptly look for consent to enter and figure out what you have to do to make the property prepared for the following inhabitant. Likewise start promoting for another inhabitant and increase the collaboration of the withdrawing occupant to demonstrate the property. Preleasing is one of the easiest approaches to build your overall gain, yet it requires some arranging and an agreeable withdrawing inhabitant that you ought to have on the off chance that you have been a persevering and reliable proprietor and have been receptive to your occupant's needs.

A rent alternative is an understanding that permits the inhabitant the privilege to buy the rented property at a foreordained cost for a specific timeframe. Merchants regularly use rent choices in moderate land markets to make extra enthusiasm for the property — even a potential purchaser right now without an initial installment has the chance to inevitably turn into a mortgage holder.

There are numerous different advantages to the investment property proprietor willing to offer a rent with a choice to buy the property. You can frequently sell the property for an incentive over the present market, and the rent alternative for the most part requires a one-time choice expense that you can keep if the purchaser doesn't practice the choice.

Additionally, the leaseholder/purchaser normally pays a higher month to month rental installment with a rent alternative in light of the fact that a part of the installment is connected to a definitive price tag. The higher regularly scheduled installments can be useful to you if the money streams for the property are as of now negative.

Investment properties taking into account seniors have dependably been famous, and the socioeconomics plainly bolster preceded with consideration regarding this progressively developing business sector specialty. Some senior properties are focusing on those needing uncommon consideration and sustenance administrations, and that is hard for some proprietors. In any case, there is a developing requirement for properties with exercises and social projects that intrigue to dynamic seniors and don't require particular abilities or noteworthy capital investments.

The control bid or initial introduction that your property gives is basic to your general achievement. By a long shot the least demanding approach to expand income and esteem is to just tidy up and address the conceded upkeep found in many properties. One of the basic standards of land is fundamental free market activity. On the other hand that your property truly emerges and looks much superior to equivalent properties, you create intense interest; your rental will remain involved at top market rents. That is the thing that income is about.

Other than restoring the straightforward conceded upkeep, another extraordinary method to expand income (and esteem) is to revamp the property. The key here is to burn through cash just on things that upgrade the property and give a fast recompense. Precedents incorporate sub-metering utilities, updating apparatuses, or including new highlights that inhabitants want.

One of the initial steps to take after you buy an investment property is to assess current working costs. See whether there's opportunity to get better, especially without adversely affecting your inhabitants.

Asking the nearby service organizations to play out a vitality review can pinpoint ways for you to lessen costs. New innovation is utilizing LED lighting, sun oriented vitality, and hydronics warming frameworks amazingly alluring. The quickly expanding expenses for water and sewer benefits in numerous regions of the nation have made the establishment of individual submeters financially savvy for distributing and recovering the expense from each occupant dependent on her genuine utilization. Separate water meters for scene regions possibly will dispense with your sewer charges if your neighborhood water utility offers them. The most ideal approach to accomplish protection of assets at your properties is to make your inhabitants legitimately in charge of their asset utilization. This lets the inhabitants control their own expenses and spares you cash.

For bigger private and business properties, solicit each from the present contractual workers and specialist co-ops to show a proposition or offer. Find other practically identical firms and at last give your business to those organizations that are safeguarded and offer the most for your dollar. As your land realm develops, you'll realize who the best esteem suppliers are, and you may find that contractual workers and specialist co-ops offer limits dependent on volume.

7.2 Investing Success in Real Estate by Ten Ways

Numerous land infomercial and class masters make it sound actually simple for anybody to make a fortune in land medium-term. Purchasing dispossessions or properties with no cash down can give attractive returns, and there's no uncertainty that the securing of land beneath its inherent esteem upgrades your odds of monetary achievement. This is essentially the conventional sage guidance (purchase low, sell high) connected to land. What's more, in the event that you can do it routinely and without issues with title, destroying physical issues, or the negative duty outcomes of being pronounced a vendor by the IRS, this technique can be very productive.

Notwithstanding, discovering great found, physically stable properties that are accessible at underneath market costs isn't basic. Our experience is that most venders realize property estimations and don't just give away their property. We frequently feel that the well-known adage "You get what you pay for" was begat by a land investor who just purchased an abandonment just to discover it has an expansive unrecorded duty lien, a substantial business inhabitant that declared financial insolvency and can void their rent, or a split section.

We would say, fruitful land investors will in general be shrewd, persevering, reliable people who eagerly perform far reaching due ingenuity before purchasing a property. They don't rethink the wheel with each arrangement, since they know their market specialty, individual abilities, and accessible assets. They have a dream and utilize their reliable course of action for every property. On the off chance that you build up these gifts, you can reveal one of a kind properties with esteem included potential that are frequently missed by your rivals.

The new land investor ought to likewise build up extra wellsprings of salary while holding or ideally notwithstanding cutting current costs; regardless of whether you can discover properties where the dealer gives all the financing, you can't get away from sure out-of-stash costs or the open door cost of lost pay as you use your time and vitality finding properties and playing out the due steadiness. We still can't seem to locate a first class land investigator or escrow organization that works for nothing.

The vast majority creates riches and accomplishes a higher expectation for everyday comforts through penance and living beneath their methods for the time being or some even do as such after they have considerable land money streams. Your inclination will rely upon your particular abilities and assets. He's ready to utilize his abilities and skill as a property director to redesign the properties, get new inhabitants, and increment the rents. Especially appealing properties are those where the present proprietor or director hasn't kept rents at the market level or that haven't been appropriately kept up cosmetically.

Continuously purchase property at the most ideal cost. This system is basic and bodes well, yet might be actually quite difficult. We propose following certain rules. When in doubt, the greater part of your land acquisitions ought to be in the fixer-upper classification and estimated as needs be. You need to purchase those properties that offer explicit difficulties that coordinate your own abilities so you can utilize your aptitudes to overhaul and upgrade the estimation of the property and increment the Net Operating Income after some time.

A land investor utilizing the "Get-Rich-Right" technique doesn't purchase another or completely redesigned property, except if it's in the way of advancement or a prime area, in light of the fact that the esteem added or thankfulness to date has just been taken by the present proprietor. These properties might be strong investments, however you're constrained to the market increments in lease and esteem as it were.

The "Get-Rich-Right" methodology relies upon discovering properties that are all around situated in the way of advancement and afterward remodeling them to expand income and esteem. In any case, don't overspend on physical enhancements. You just need to make those remodels or updates that expansion the allure of the property to your objective market. Your property is a rental unit, not your very own home. You might need to put premium ledges and machines in your home, yet you can't get a decent profit for your investment on the off chance that you over improve your rentable house. Pride of proprietorship is significant, however you're maintaining a business and overspending on one property will constrain your capacity to set aside the following up front installment and fabricate your portfolio and accomplish riches.

CHAPTER 8: GOALS TO REACHING TOP

8.1 Ascertain the Base Camp

The principal arrange in structure a money related track to keep running on is to set up your budgetary base camp. The way to this is to fuse the Net worth Model into your life. The initial step is to make an individual spending plan and stick to it. This will enable you to ensure you don't burn through the entirety of your cash and will have some to contribute. An individual spending will move you to live well—yet well beneath your moderate methods until your budgetary riches has been amassed. By following a spending you will start to comprehend why you purchase costly things after you become well off and not previously. At last you'll come to comprehend that the initial step to turning into a tycoon is to carry on with a controlled-utilization way of life. The second step in setting up your budgetary base camp is to keep a continuous total assets worksheet: your riches building scorecard.

Designate an hour every week to looking it over and posing one inquiry: "How might I become my total assets and income?" Each time you buy something, you will start to come to an obvious conclusion regarding what you do with cash and the manner in which it influences your money related riches. After some time you will come to comprehend why tycoons state that money related riches isn't equivalent to earned salary and that sparing isn't equivalent to investing. The last advance in structure your base camp is to stay away from obligation. In spite of the fact that this is easy to state, it is difficult to do. Try to make a promise to abstain from financing your own expenses of living. Tragically, numerous individuals get enveloped with an "obtain and purchase" way of life. Tycoons do the definite inverse, receiving the mantra "set aside, at that point purchase," particularly for real buys. Try not to give your credit a chance to card do your putting something aside for you. When in doubt, attempt to pay with money or money comparable. At the end of the day, treat your charge card like money and pay off the equalization every month. Moguls don't utilize obligation conveying plastic credit.

They have no enthusiasm for paying high intrigue, and neither do you. In the event that you can, purchase based on "needs" and maintains a strategic distance from a "needs" acquiring way of life. When something breaks, dependably think "fix" first, "utilized" second, and "new" last. You will probably maintain a strategic distance from non-resource based obligation no matter what. However, at last, on the other hand that you should bring about obligation; attempt to ensure that the obligation term and resource life span coordinate.

8.2 Protecting Future

The primary activity to secure your future is to spare three to a half year of everyday costs for a just-in-case account. You need a security net so regardless of what happens you have alternatives. Expect this hold add up to go up as your total assets goes up.

Next, buy a home. This not exclusively is constrained reserve funds, it likewise verifies the one resource that decides your way of life more than some other. Similarly as with some other buy, purchase based on necessities first and needs second. Purchase what you want to manage, not what a bank will loan you. Purchase in view of your family's arrangements. Don't "under buy," requiring a move too early, or "overbuy," foreseeing more salary later on. It's a tight line to walk, yet you should walk it. On the off chance that you do "under buy," you presumably will finish up making this your first investment property. "Overbuy" and it may place you in the poorhouse. Try not to progress toward becoming "house rich and pay poor." The genuine key to opportunity here lies in putting your installments on a quick way to owning your home without a worry in the world.

Third, ensure your future by protecting it in key territories. You will require sufficient handicap protection to secure a base way of life. You will require satisfactory disaster protection to help bolster your family and settle any bequest government expenses. You will require the best reasonable medical coverage for you and your family. You will require satisfactory substitution esteem and obligation protection for your home, vehicle, and individual property. In the event that you get your protection specialist, bookkeeper, and home arranging lawyer together, you ought to have the option to make sense of this in about 60 minutes. At last, make a bequest plan. It must incorporate straightforward however painstakingly considered element arranging, suitable trusts and wills, and methodologies to limit or wipe out legacy imposes and amplify lender assurance. The investment you make from the get-go for the administrations of an astounding bequest arranging lawyer will at last profit. At the point when Sam Walton was a young fellow simply beginning in business and could least bear the cost of it, he set up his bequest plan. Subsequently, toward a mind-blowing finish one of the best close to home fortunes at any point amassed was exchanged to his beneficiaries with practically zero duties paid. Moguls get this, thus should you?

8.3 Future Funding

It's a great opportunity to turn into an investor. To accomplish this you need to do what investors do: get cash and way it, pick the land showcase you need to put resources into and learn it, and fabricate your work and leads arranges and create them. School is never out for the fruitful. Be clear about your "must-center" territories and ace them. Keep in mind, you figure out how to win before you specialty to get rich. Set up together a perusing list every year and read those books. What's more, do likewise for instructional sound tapes, recordings and DVDs. Go to one class a year about a point you have to know better. Spend time with your system individuals and tune in to their experience and exhortation. Most significant, wake up each day and state, I'm an investor. Today could be the day I discover a chance and make an arrangement."

With cash, information, and connections behind you, it's an ideal opportunity to produce investment opportunity leads. To start with, put your Criteria down on paper. In the event that they're not recorded, you most likely don't have them. Next, retain this rundown with the goal that it winds up like a tune in your mind you can't resist recalling. Presently go prospect and market for leads that meet your Criteria. Pick a couple of techniques and give them sufficient opportunity to check whether they will work. Since your Criteria, specialty, and target geographic market make a remarkable equation, you should work with your lead age approach for some time to start to see unsurprising outcomes. Time-obstruct your schedule for lead age time and secure that time. Set the objective of creating a lead multi day, put those leads into your database, and afterward work them.

Suspects and prospects are totally unique. One won't, and one will. One squanders your time, and one merits your time. One costs you cash, and one profits. One does not merit any exertion, and one merits all the exertion. Try to have the option to make sense of rapidly which will be which. When you can do that, you're doing the absolute most basic work investors do. You'll pick your prospects by reviewing the property, meeting the dealer, and getting your system included. You will probably have the option to state, "My prospects are looking into." You'll have the option to state this when you think about a property that meets your Criteria and is claimed by a dealer who will meet your Terms.

8.4 Staying at Course

The last phase of structure your money related track is to make and continue vitality with the goal that you can finish what has been started. Try not to stress over the economy or the market. Warren Buffett says he doesn't. It's your Criteria that issue, not the conditions that may make their accessibility. Adhere to your arrangement and contribute based on your Criteria. The diagram beneath lays the particular methodology you should take. You should commit around 10 hours per week to this riches building program. You can complete a little every day, or you can complete seven days merits each end of the week. The decision is yours. Simply remain on course.

As direct as this looks, executing it very well may challenge. Effective investing and riches building is a procedure, not an occasion. It's a perseverance race, not a snappy dash, and you should make and store vitality to run it. Burnout prowls behind each property you should go see and each merchant you should meet and consult with. You can't stand to give this a chance to transpire. You should prepare for exhaustion and diversions with the goal that you can keep investing and getting a charge out of it. It's a whole deal, and in the event that you don't keep with it, you will be bamboozling your investment plan and yourself. You'll require vitality intend to progress toward becoming and remain a mogul investor.

CONCLUSION

Investing in rentable houses can create current pay and noteworthy tax cuts just as fabricate value from increase throughout the years and decades. Give specific consideration to your month to month spending plan and ensure that you have sufficient protection inclusion. Best land investors fabricate their land investment portfolio through setting aside some cash and afterward bit by bit purchasing properties throughout the years.

Land is the main investment that we are aware of that you can live in or lease to deliver salary. You can likewise determine vast duty free benefits when you sell your vital living arrangement at a more expensive rate than you paid for it. Territories, where new improvement or redevelopment is going, are the place you need to be. The best land investment properties are ones that are very much found and physically stable yet cosmetically tested and ineffectively oversaw.

While The Real Estate Investor is a handbook for investing in land, it is additionally—at its center—a manual for making money related riches. Making budgetary riches starts with a comprehension of the best dependable standards for profiting. Making riches is tied in with perceiving that riches and wealth are not the equivalent, that the hole between a decent arrangement and an incredible arrangement is a huge gap made by an absence of intelligence. Learning the distinction can change the manner in which you take a gander at the world, and in the end it can change a mind-blowing state.

As you'll find, The Real Estate Investor is extremely two books in one. The initial segment is given to your reasoning. In that part you'll defy a portion of your legends about cash, land, and yourself. You'll additionally become familiar with some immortal realities about the manner in which cash works. On the off chance that you can figure out how to take on a similar mindset as a tycoon, you'll have a vastly improved opportunity to wind up one. The second piece of the book is tied in with making a move. It's the "how-to" part and will plot a demonstrated way to pursue just as tried models to utilize.

www.ingramcontent.com/pod-product-compliance
Lightning Source LLC
Chambersburg PA
CBHW072131170526
45158CB00004BA/1324